José Cárdenas Pallares

A POOR MAN CALLED JESUS

REFLECTIONS ON THE GOSPEL OF MARK

Translated from the Spanish by Robert R. Barr

ORBIS BOOKS

Maryknoll, New York 10545

The Catholic Foreign Mission Society of America (Maryknoll) recruits and trains people for overseas missionary service. Through Orbis Books Maryknoll aims to foster the international dialogue that is essential to mission. The books published, however, reflect the opinions of their authors and are not meant to represent the official position of the society.

Originally published as *Un pobre llamado Jesús: Relectura del Evangelio de Marcos,* copyright © 1982 by Casa Unida de Publicaciones, Mexico City

Manuscript editor: Mary J. Heffron

Library of Congress Cataloging in Publication Data

Cárdenas Pallares, José
  A poor man called Jesus.

  Translation of: Pobre llamado Jesús.
  Bibliography: p.
  Includes index.
  1. Bible. N.T. Mark—Criticism, interpretation, etc. I. Title.
BS2585.2.C3413 1986   226'.306   85-15339
ISBN 0-88344-398-8 (pbk.)

Contents

Preface vi

Introduction: The Sad State of Biblical Studies 1

Chapter 1: Jesus' Conflicts 5
A New Point of View: Jesus' Word 5
Disturbing Deeds of Liberation 9
A Religion of Hope and Gladness 14
The Sacred Right of the Poor 20
Under Surveillance 23
Parallels in Luke's Gospel 25
The Human Being as above All Law 26
Abolition of All Manner of Discrimination 26

Chapter 2: Jesus' Power and Strength 28
Miracles 28
God's Language for Everybody 28
Signs of Liberation 29
Good News for the Downtrodden 31
Signs of an Abundance of Love 34
Signs in the Community 38
*Signs of Service and of Relationship with the
    Father* 39
Jesus in League with Satan? 41
A Strange Person 41
A Strange Community 42
Subverting the Prevailing Order 43
Rejection and Repression 45

Chapter 3: Jesus and the Oppressed 47
Jesus and Woman 47
Women in the Time of Jesus 47

iii

Christians and Women   51

What Is a Poor Person Worth?   56

*What Is of Real Value: God in the Hearts of the
    Poor   56*

*"I Want You to Observe": The Gulf Is
    Unbridgeable   58*

Chapter 4: Confrontation with the Powers   **60**

Jesus and Wealth   60

Skirting the Issue: The Interpreters   60

Scriptural Meaning of "Rich"   63

Meaning of "Rich" in Hellenized Judaism   64

A Rich Person? Impossible!   66

God or Money?   68

*The Way of the Cross: Complete
    Renunciation   69*

Jesus and Power   72

The Interests at Stake   72

"To God What Is God's"   75

Behind the Mask of Holiness   76

Front Seats in the Synagogue   76

Devouring the Savings of Widows   78

Remain the Last One of All   79

Chapter 5: The Way of the Cross   **80**

Let's Talk about a Murder   80

The Agony   80

The Arrest   83

The Trial   86

Peter's Denial   93

Jesus before Pilate   94

Chapter 6: And They Crucified Him   **102**

The Crucified One   102

Jesus' Death   106

Chapter 7: The Resurrection   **117**

Differences in the Accounts   117

Heart and Soul in the Telling   118

Structure of Mark's Account   119
Similar Forms   120
No Rising without a Passion   123
   The Rising of the Accursed One   123
   Invalid Testimony   124
   Call to the Deserters   124
An Unpredictable God   124
Liberation from Every Encumbrance   126
Triumph of Life   126

Works Cited   **131**

Preface

On May 1, 1978, in Guadalajara I addressed a group of people belonging to basic Christian communities, on the subject of Jesus' conflicts. I had devoted a great deal of thought and research to the subject. I was greatly concerned about the saccharine, colorless image of Jesus that has been propagated among us and that causes so many problems of conscience for Christians involved in popular struggles. My reflections on these issues became chapter 1 of this book.

About the same time I was asked to speak about the Passion of our Lord to the lay apostles of the diocese of Colima, a predominantly rural and semirural community, at their Lenten meeting. I selected the oldest text, Mark's Gospel, which was written among a marginalized people in the language of the poor. It seemed to me that my own people were like Mark's audience. The subject of the Passion fascinated me. I saw that the whole Gospel of Mark was oriented to the Passion and murder of Jesus and that only in the light of these occurrences could one understand what this Gospel was communicating to us about Jesus. After my talks I continued to ruminate on and study my subject matter, and eventually I completely reworked my approach to Jesus' trial before Pilate and to his crucifixion and death.

I continued to think about the Passion of Jesus. During the summer of 1980 I drafted my thoughts—found in chapter 5—on Jesus' agony. In November of the same year, during a brief stay in Laredo, Texas, I saw peasants arrested as wetbacks, and the attitude of compromise taken by so many believers in the face of the suffering of the poor was painful and puzzling to me. I put the finishing touches to the sections on Jesus' arrest and Peter's denial.

In 1978 the aspirants of Armonía Convent in Colima asked me to speak to them on Jesus' attitude toward women. The talks I gave evolved into "Jesus and Woman."

In May 1979 the Bible groups and basic Christian communities of Agua Prieta, Sonora, asked me to help them in their reflections on Jesus. They had been exposed to "mass-produced miracles" stamped "made in USA," and were tempted either to set aside completely the gospel accounts of Jesus' miracles or, worse, to succumb to credulousness and enthusiasm where the new "miracles" were concerned. It was for them that I worked up the topic of Jesus' power.

For these same groups I developed the subject of Jesus accused of being in league with Satan. I saw so many church people, Catholics and Protestants, branding these groups (yesterday as today) as "infiltrated" or "atheistic" or whatever the trendy epithet happened to be. Before the assassination of Archbishop Oscar Arnulfo Romero of El Salvador, I had worked out the ideas contained in the section entitled "Jesus in League with Satan?" and I finished writing it by Holy Week of 1980.

Toward the end of November 1975, the National Biblical Encounter was held in Guadalajara. I received the assignment of expounding upon two subjects in an elegant school before an audience of mostly very comfortable people. One of the subjects was Jesus and the rich. After my presentation the audience was furious. They assured me that I had injured their faith. If the Inquisition had still been functioning, they would have had me sent to the bonfire! My talk was later published in *Contacto,* a periodical published by the Mexican Social Secretariat. Time passed, but the war-horse was still pawing the earth, and a number of friends of mine asked me to approach this subject once more, with more calm and more scholarly apparatus. And so in July 1979 I "gave birth" to the section entitled "Jesus and Wealth."

The subject of Jesus and power flows logically from the subject of Jesus and wealth. Power and riches always go in tandem; when Christians suffer the oppression of the rich, they also suffer the repression of the powerful. Mark 12:13–17 has been so distorted that the wealthy themselves were asking me for an explanation! In chapter 4 I attempt to offer that explanation.

Without Jesus' Resurrection the Gospel would be truncated and sterile. During a sabbatical I worked out the subject of the last chapter, the Resurrection. This was toward the end of October 1979.

In early March 1980 I developed the material contained in "Behind the Mask of Holiness" and in "What Is a Poor Person Worth?" I have written these sections with the class division within the church in mind. These sections are my tribute to the many poor who have helped me in my faith.

Many friends in the state of Colima, the cities of Juárez and Agua Prieta, the south of Jalisco, and so many other places have asked me to publish this material. Reverend Rubén Castañeda especially showed great interest in my reflections. I have selected the subjects treated in this book because they reveal the human and radical element in Jesus' struggles. They show the liberating character of his praxis and God's wholehearted partiality toward the oppressed. The cause of Jesus is the cause of a God who is inseparably united with all the exploited. The God of Jesus, and Jesus himself, are, before all else, liberation, measureless love, hope, and life.

Introduction: The Sad State of Biblical Studies

These pages are the fruit of a very disconcerting experience. I arrived in the parish of Guadalupe, in Manzanillo, Colima, quite confident in the knowledge I had acquired in lecture halls. I was convinced that all I had to do was pass on to the people what I had learned and that this would mature into their own Christian commitment. I was full of enthusiasm for the mission of instructing the ignorant. *O sancta simplicitas!* In the first place, I learned more than I taught; furthermore, what I taught was of very little interest to anyone.

The problem of biblical exegesis has always been how to make God's Word accessible to the contemporary human being. But this human being does not exist among us. Or, worse still, he or she is identified, at least in the mind of the poor, with the oppressor—with the one who treats the poor as beasts of burden or as curiosities in a zoo.

In our own day—not in the Dark Ages, but in our own day—half the human race are illiterate and two-thirds are hungry. The shacks of our slums are as real today as are the ultra-modern residences of the rich (and the latter are the cause of the former). Torture is not old-fashioned—it is more in style every day, and the ones who have to suffer it are the poor and those who struggle at the side of the poor.

Who are more modern: the ones subjected to inhuman treatment or the ones behind the desks washing their hands of the whole matter? Can the hopes of those who have everything be the same as the hopes of those who have nothing and who are treated as if they were nothing? Can their problems and concerns be identical? Can the gospel be first and foremost a proclamation of good news to the satisfied? What project afoot in society—or more modestly, what manner of pastoral activity—will give us the key to our exegesis?

Jesus was a poor person, and he was committed to the poorest of the poor from the crown of his head to the soles of his feet. He spoke the language of the poor. He felt the sorrows and joys of the poor, and he met death in a manner reserved for the poor. Are we modern-day interpreters of the Bible on Jesus' wavelength? Has our sociological condition any affinity with his? Or is our position more like that of the ruling Pharisees or the Sadducees? One of the indicators of our lack of harmony with Jesus has to do with language—our language is complicated, but Jesus' language was simple. Saddest of all, we are not even concerned about the difference.

The gospels arose in communities of the poor: "Not many of you are wise, as men account wisdom; not many are influential; and surely not many are wellborn. God chose those whom the world considers absurd . . . " (1 Cor 1:26–27). Furthermore, the gospels arose in communities of the oppressed (James 2:6–7). To us today, strong words like those of James 5:1–6 sound like demagogy and seem contrary to the scientific spirit. The language of Saint Mark's Gospel is a simple language. Mark's Gospel is poor people's literature. But today, to study the Bible "seriously" one needs a great deal of leisure and a great deal of money. Study of this type requires an investment that is not only beyond the means of most individual Christians but, in an underdeveloped country, is beyond the means of almost every community. This being the case, what kind of "wisdom" may I expect from a poor person's study of the gospels?

The first Christians fell under cruel attack from imperial might. For them the Roman Empire was a destructive beast. Today, Sacred Scripture is studied with the benevolent approval of the *pax imperialis;* no exegetical activity disturbs the tranquility of the "empire" for a single moment. What biblical periodical has ever fallen under any suspicion of being subversive? Biblical specialists have curiously little to suffer from the Neros and Domitians of our time. But neither do their studies instill light and strength in Christians persecuted by the lords of this world.

Hence the imperative need of finding other perspectives. We Christians, who live today in a world of oppression and dehumanization, cannot afford the luxury of devoting all our energies to the awkward limitation of the intellectual exploits—and fancy foot-work—of Christians who live worlds away. Their achievements seem artificial indeed in the face of the brutal facts of the misery and calamities in the modern world.

Job's cries were not very coherent, and they were not the remedy for his sorrow. It may be the same with the commentaries in this book. I have no wish to deceive the reader: this book arises from the dark belly of the underdeveloped world, from the marginalized neighborhoods of a backward, exploited country. The stigma of being backward weighs not only on the writings, but on the writer as well.

Chapter 1

Jesus' Conflicts

Jesus' whole public career, from start to finish, is cast in a framework of disputes and confrontations with the intellectual and spiritual leaders of his people (Mk 2:1–12, 12:36–40). The framework reveals not only the kind of opposition Jesus faced, but also the subversive nature of his activity and teaching. Consequently, it reveals the cause of his violent death.

The framework of conflict in which Jesus' activity and teaching is set shows us that that activity and teaching were themselves conflictual, that they were calculated to incite conflict. It shows us that Jesus stood then, as he stands today, in stark opposition to those who control the conscience and the life of peoples.

The Gospel of Mark reports the first block of controversies, and we are struck by their contrived arrangement—their artificial order. Mark gives us five reports in sharply escalating degrees of antagonism: from secret criticism (2:6), to complaints lodged with Jesus' disciples (2:16), to challenges made to Jesus' face (2:18, 24), to keeping "an eye on" him (3:2), to the conspiracy between the Pharisees and the Herodians to kill him (3:6).

An examination of this series of conflictual occurrences will enable us to understand why, to what end, Jesus carried on his struggle.

A NEW POINT OF VIEW: JESUS' WORD

In the first report (Mk 2:1–12), we learn about the healing of a paralytic. What is important in this account is not the miracle, but Jesus' words accompanying the act of healing and the interpretation of his act that these words provide us. The account relates the circumstances of the act tersely, but the words are enough to make us see what Jesus is claiming.

Jesus is stirring up a popular movement. "They began to gather in great numbers. There was no longer any room for them, even around the door" (Mk 2:2). (We see the same thing reported in Mark 1:45, 3:20, 4:1, 5:21, and 6:31.) We see a throng of poor rushing out to meet another who is poor. The house where Jesus is lodging is a humble one, without any porch or vestibule. Its door leads directly to the street. It is a shack and so its roof is easy to dismantle. It has a flat roof covered over with earth, nothing more. Such is the place where one might come to meet Jesus and where a miraculous cure is performed. The place where the power of God will be made manifest is a poor person's hut. This is where Jesus' word will be heard.

The paralytic utters not a single word. Four people carry him to the little house on a primitive pallet, a stretcher. They open a hole in the roof and let the stretcher down through it into the house. The patient is a poor person. He is carried on a cot, and not a fancy one: the Greek word for it is *krábbatos,* "a humble pallet" (Moulton and Mulligan 1963, 357).

All through the Gospel of Mark we find an atmosphere of faith in search of help, faith seeking to make the impossible possible (see Mk 5:34, 7:28, 9:14–29, 10:48, and 11:22 [Pesch 1976, 1:155]).

Jesus is confronted with a body laid low, a body wasting away. The very act of piercing the roof is an act of confidence in Jesus' ability to help. Jesus sees the faith of these people. Faith, in Mark's Gospel is the opposite of cowardice. It is the courage to be with Jesus, the certitude that with him we cannot lose (Mk 4:40). It is confidence in Jesus' power (5:34, 10:32), not in sterile, oppressive practices.

Jesus' words to the paralytic are words that have never before been heard. "My son," he says "your sins are forgiven." Jesus bestows on the paralytic the gift of unconditional forgiveness. The case is different from that of the prophet Nathan, who merely *knew* that someone's sins had been forgiven. Jesus *authoritatively declares* that someone's sins have been forgiven. Emergence from a situation of sin—a life free of faults—was the people's great hope

(Jer 31:31–34; Ez 16:62–63, 36:25–29). It was the sign that new times had come (Acts 2:38, 5:31). Effecting this emergence from sin, this situation of sinlessness, was the exclusive prerogative of God (Is 43:25, 44:22).

But Jesus begins to collide with power and authority. The rabbis could accept Jesus as Master, as teacher—why not?—provided his power were a power like their own. But it is not. There are no bookish discussions here. This is no scholastic disputation. It is a new order, a completely new evaluation of events and attitude (Minnette de Tillesse 1968, 155). Jesus' attitude shocks. It provokes scandal among and opposition from the educated. As a matter of principle, they could not brook the possibility of deliverance from physical paralysis.

So they accuse Jesus of blasphemy. To blaspheme meant to place the power of God on the same level as that of the pagan idols or beneath that of the great persons of this world (2 Kgs 18:28–38); it also meant to deny the saving power of the Lord (Is 53:5), or to place oneself on the same level with God (Jn 10:33) (Beyer 1964–76a, 1:621–25). The academicians refer to Jesus with contempt, calling him "the man." In accusing him of blasphemy, they are taking the first steps toward putting him to death as an enemy of God.

Jesus' accusers are the intelligentsia, the educated, those schooled in the Law (Ezr 7:6, 11)—the experts in tradition, the people who know things the common run of mortals cannot know (Jeremias 1964–76a, 1:740–42). They make science and God into instruments of power. They dazzle the poor, ignorant people with their prestige. They dominate people's consciences: "Woe to you lawyers! You have taken away the key of knowledge. You yourselves have not gained access, yet you have stopped those who wished to enter!" (Lk 11:52). People's concrete situation is of no importance to them. Indeed they take unfair advantage of the abandoned and the ignorant (Lk 11:46). Their knowledge is the occasion of their vainglory, and an opportunity for self-enrichment (Lk 20:46–47). They are hypocrites; they are inconsistent. In their practice they set honor to God and responsibility toward those in need in mutual opposition. Adroitly they annul the demands of God's love (Mk 7:9–13).

No one else at that time would pronounce judgment upon them, it seems. They are ordained rabbis, the people's leaders. They are renowned, respected scholars. Their tombs are to be adjacent to those of the prophets. Then suddenly Jesus' praxis shows them in another light. For Jesus they are not the successors of the prophets. Honor paid to them is honor paid to the dead (Lk 11:47–51). To their transmission of dead, meaningless words, Jesus contrasts nearness to the living God (Mt 5:21–48).

We are faced with a different view of God and human beings here. Jesus relates forgiveness of sin and faith to the liberation of people's bodies. Jesus grants God's pardon—deliverance from all the burdens and failures of the past—to a person who, in society's eyes, is of no value. According to the scribes, God is indifferent to the suffering of such a person.

Jesus gives himself the title Son of Man. This was not a messianic title. The Messiah awaited by the lawyers and by those who had adopted their thinking was a Messiah associated and identified with power (Book of Henoch; Qumran *War Scroll,* Odes of Solomon, Fourth Book of Ezra).

The title Son of Man occurs frequently in the Book of Daniel, where it goes hand in hand with *true* power—with the manifestation of the imperishable reign of God—in contrast to the power of the monstrous beasts, the empires. The power of the Son of Man—hence the power of Jesus—is the opposite of oppressive power (Dn 4:14, 34; 7:14).

The evangelist, following Jesus, uses the miracle of the healing of the paralytic to confront us with a question: Whose side is God on? Is God on the side of the one who frees people's bodies or on the side of those who do nothing to help people escape their paralysis? In Jesus the power of God is shown to stand in opposition to the power of certain human beings. Indeed, all the controversies in Jesus' life are a proclamation that his power is superior to the power of David (Mk 2:25), that it brings joy (2:19), that it extricates human beings from their humiliating situation, and that it is the power by which the will of God becomes reality (3:4). To oppose Jesus' practice is to oppose the will of God. What is at stake here is not this or that interpretation of a particular passage in Sacred Scripture. What is at stake here is the acceptance either of a God who is on the side of human beings, especially human beings in need, or of a God whose back is turned on human pain.

DISTURBING DEEDS OF LIBERATION

Jesus attempted to do more than simply teach truths. If his activity were reducible to this, there would be nothing novel about it. Rejected by the lawyers, Jesus invites someone the lawyers reject, someone all society rejects, to form part of his company (Mk 2:14).

The person he invites does not reject him. The tax collector accepts Jesus, even though Jesus has been judged a blasphemer (2:7) and is therefore in danger of being excluded from the people of Israel and from life (Lv 24:10–16).

It is what Jesus *does* that calls the lawyers' attention to him and provokes their indignation. Jesus dines with social garbage; he loves to pass the time with society's outcasts (Mk 2:15–17). He takes his meals with society's most contemptible persons, and we are told that this earns him the lawyers' reproach (Mk 2:16). This is the first passage in Mark's Gospel in which the disciples are mentioned. It is Jesus, not they, who is reproached, but the reproach is intended to discredit him in their eyes.

Jesus consorts with publicans, tax collectors, and sinners. And he consorts with them as if it went without saying that he should. Neither in the narrative parts of the account nor in Jesus' words as this account transmits them to us is there any idealizing of these friends of his. To these truly lost, derelict people Jesus concretely demonstrates his friendship and respect.

Pagan and Jew alike saw tax collectors as contemptible and held them in the worst regard. Lucian puts them in the same category with adulterers, sycophants, informers, and pimps (Taylor 1966, 204). Palestine, like any land subject to the Roman Empire, groaned under the burden of all manner of taxation. There were agricultural taxes—in money and in kind—income taxes, investment taxes, rent taxes, transportation taxes, a census tax, and so on and on. These taxes were indispensable to the Roman civil administration and consequently to the Pax Romana, that "peace" or state of pacification whose main benefits fell to the powerful. Those who gathered the taxes (*publicani,* in Latin) were obliged to hand over the actual amount of the tax to the state, of course, but they themselves could collect more than the amount legally levied.

Almost until the time of Nero practically no one even knew what the official tax rates were. The greed of some tax collectors knew no bounds. They abused their prerogatives for their personal emolument.

Judaism put the publicans in the same category as petty thieves. Publicans had a reputation for extortion, slander, false denunciation, and like abuses. Their ritual impurity was beyond question. None could be admitted to the pharisaic confraternities. For a devout Jew, tax collectors were on a level with gamblers, usurers, shepherds, slaves, and the violent (Jeremias 1977, 322). They were the lost sheep of Israel (Mt 10:6, 15:24). Publicans were the pus of a rotten society that believed itself whole. They were toadies—they had to pass the money they collected on to somebody above them. In all cases they had to serve the interests of the affluent.

According to the pharisaic ethic, the sinner, the *rasha'*, was the opposite of the wise person, the *hakam*. The *hasid*, pious, good person, was the one who studied the teachings of the Law (Pirqe Avot 5:10–19). Only constant converse with the Law could safeguard one from sin (Qiddushim 1:10). Ignorance of the Law was the equivalent of sin (Sanhedrin 8:5). Accordingly, anyone not devoted to a study of the Law was the dwelling-place of sin: "This lot, that knows nothing about the law . . . are lost anyway" (Jn 7:49). The same was to be said of all who did not follow the pharisaic interpretation of the Law (Jn 9:16, 24–25, 31). All these persons sinned—by their ignorance, whether they wished to or not—and hence their early death was desirable lest they continue sinning and "deliver themselves to the increase of their fault" (Sanhedrin 8:5).

Sinner, then, became more than a moral term. It became a social one as well. The renowned Rabbi Hallel said: "An ignorant person does not fear sin, and an *'am ha'arets* is not devout" (Pirqe Avot 2:5). *'Am ha'arets*—literally, "people of the earth," the common people, those lacking in education—were denied all social consideration (Rengstorf 1964–76, 1:317–33). They deserved no relief. For pagans, shepherds, or goatherds there was no way off the treadmill (Jeremias 1977, 3). In a complicated moral system where one's neighbor is not the indispensable locus of the encounter with God the masses of the poor are necessarily sinners.

Jesus subverts the social code. He breaks down the barriers. He refuses to seek the status of a lawyer. He makes himself an outcast. He forms his social ties with the refuse of society. In Jesus' dealings, in Jesus' gladness, society's rubbish finds its own gladness. Jesus shakes the legal order to its foundations.

The primitive Christian community cannot have invented this. Like the rabbis, it relegated publicans to the same category as pagans, and contradistinguished them from the sons and daughters of the kingdom—for example in Matthew 5:46–47 or 18:15–20 (Pesch 1976, 162–67).

Publicans and pagans are the people who constitute Jesus' milieu. This is the class he belongs to. "This man cannot be from God because he does not keep the sabbath. . . .We know this man is a sinner" the Pharisees say (Jn 9:16, 24). They treat him as a glutton and a drunkard (Mt 11:19). They are scandalized at Jesus' conduct (Lk 11:37–38) (Rengstorff 1964–76). According to the official norm and official religious decency, Jesus is an outlaw. At the same time, Jesus, by his conduct, challenges this very norm, this decency, and the whole ideological world underlying it. The lawyers challenge Jesus' behavior because they feel challenged themselves.

Jesus' reply, we are told, is: "People who are healthy do not need a doctor; sick people do. I have come to call sinners, not the self-righteous" (Mk 2:17). Some commentators maintain that the first part of this reply is not an authentic logion of Jesus; or at least, they say, Jesus did not make this statement at this particular time and place. Others maintain that the first part of the statement is authentic but not the second. However the case may be, at the very least this declaration has its origin in the primitive Christian community. But the attitudes and practice of that community cannot be explained except by reference to the practice of Jesus. Thus before all else we must ask ourselves: If the logion is not authentic, then what made the community place such strong words in Jesus' mouth? What led this rural community to split away from the legal framework that was the very marrow of their being?

In the first part of the reply, the topic is not the doctor but the people who are sick. The accent falls not on the person of the doctor but on the situation of the patients. Now *illness* or *sickness* in the language of the Old Testament, besides denoting a physi-

cal ailment, could also be used to mean any of the following:
(1) dereliction, oppression, misery (Is 57:18–19, 61:1; Jer 14:9);
(2) national crisis, the decomposition of the nation (Hos 5:13, 6:1);
(3) apostasy, repugnance for the truth, sin, the root of evil (Jer 3:
22, 30:17). In all these cases reference is to suffering, misery,
calamity.

The response attributed to Jesus was a familiar proverb of Greek
antiquity. Parallels in Judaism have not been discovered (Dupont
1969, 2:228). Jesus' use of the proverb must not be understood in a
general way. It must be understood in context. It is a kind of
parable. Jesus is seeking to explain his attitude toward sinners.
The only thing Jesus is interested in is in bestowing "health"
—salvation—on those who are in a situation of suffering. All other
concerns are irrelevant. Jesus cannot be indifferent to human
humiliation. He dines with publicans and sinners because they are
the ones in need of relief; they are the ones who need emergency
assistance.

Jesus healed the paralyzed person (Mk 2:10) and sinners
(2:15–17). The same Jesus who bestows health bestows joy. The
purpose of his activity is to heal—to do away with situations that
cause suffering. What counts for Jesus, as for a physician, is the
situation of people's suffering. His mission is in the service of these
people. Their objective situation must be changed. Jesus' task
consists in suppressing evil and misery, and nothing can be
forbidden him when it is a question of fulfilling his task. Jesus'
cause bears no resemblance to a religiousness that is unconcerned
with changing the situation of the marginalized human being.

In the second part of Jesus' reply—"I have come to call sinners,
not the self-righteous" (some manuscripts add, as does Luke
5:32, "[call sinner] to a change of heart")—the contraposition of
"sinners" and "righteous" places us in a Palestinian context.
(Jesus does not say "*self*-righteous," as our translation would have
it. He comes right out and says "righteous," *dikaious*. Jesus does
not use the words *righteous* and *sinners* in an ironical way, so as to
become entangled in a question of language.)

Jesus adopts the viewpoint and language of his adversaries
[our translation, by the insertion of "self," does not altogether respect this] in order to establish common grounds for

an understanding of his own viewpoint. Jesus knows that [the righteous] have acquitted themselves of a great many obligations (Lk 15:29)—that they have been constant in their observance (Mt 20:12), and that they have taken their obligations to heart (Lk 18:11–12). Nor does he attempt to minimize the moral misery of "sinners" (Lk 15:12–17). The sinner's debt is ten times greater than that of the just person (Lk 7:41:–43) [Dupont 1969, 2:228].

Yes, Jesus admits the righteousness of his adversaries. To be sure, they fulfill all the requirements of the pharisaic interpretation of the Law. But after that they are inconsistent. In Jesus' view there are hypocrites and criminals among the righteous (Mt 23:28); there are trap-setters and intriguers (Lk 20:20).

The evil in this righteousness is that it goes hand in hand with self-complacency (Lk 18:11) and presumption (Mk 12:38–39). It does not take the will of God seriously (Mt 21:29, 23:23). Instead it seeks to have God at its own service (Lk 15:2, 28). Accordingly, this righteousness is without value in God's eyes (Mt 23:13; Lk 18:14). Hence Jesus not only condemns this "righteousness" (Mt 21:32, Lk 7:30), but also invites his disciples to go beyond it (Mt 5:20). Jesus criticizes all legal observance, all rectitude, that does not lead to complete dedication, that does not make a commitment to the poor (Mk 7, 10:21–31). Nothing can have equal value with the demands of the liberating love proclaimed by Jesus (Lk 12:5; Mt 8:21–22). Jesus stands against everything that sets aside God's Law and prevents a person from making concrete decisions in favor of the lowly.

But there is more. Jesus not only embraces the cause of the outcast, he also makes himself an outcast. In dealing with publicans as he does, Jesus joins the lower classes (Pesch 1970, 15–17). The lifestyle he creates makes no provision for exclusions. Those who have no place in society have a surprise in store: in God's plan, which has become visible in Jesus, there is place for them indeed.

Jesus grants forgiveness, not only by his words (Mk 2:5–10) but by his deeds as well. Jesus' forgiveness is the power to demolish whatever excludes people from acceptance. Jesus' friendship with sinners demonstrates his power to forgive. Jesus has not come to reinforce society's barriers but to overthrow them. Hence it is precisely to the rejected that he commits himself. Jesus' power is at the service of men and women who are thoroughly marginalized. He is the messenger who delivers the invitation (Mt 22:1–14; Lk 14:16–24) to the joy of the kingdom (Pesch 1970, 15–17). It is precisely the poor, the crippled, the lame, the blind—in other words, the excluded—who accept this invitation to joy. Jesus' power has as its mission the suppression of the affront to the lowly. To follow Jesus means to become a brother or sister to the excluded (Lk 2:14ff).

In a word, the controversies in Mark's Gospel show us Jesus' power being at the service of human liberty (Mk 2:23–28), a power committed to the abolition of the insult (2:15–17), humiliation, and suffering (3:1–6) inflicted on human beings.

A RELIGION OF HOPE AND GLADNESS

Not all of the lawyers were Pharisees, but the majority of them were. Likewise, not all Pharisees were lawyers, but their leaders and more influential colleagues were (Jeremias 1977, 261ff.). Lawyers were the authorized interpreters of the Law, and they were the ordained rabbis. Pharisees were members of a pious association, a prayer community, characterized by works of philanthropy and the observance of the liturgical precepts. They accorded special importance to good works—prayer, tithing, almsgiving, and fasting—over and above the commandments of the Law, and they believed those good works could augment their personal merit. The social composition of the group varied, but most Pharisees were lower middle-class (Jeremias 1977, 273).

Politically the Pharisees were oportunists. They had called on the Syrian king Demetrius III for aid against Alexander Jannaeus and had allied themselves with Demetrius' widow, who had shown herself to be favorable to them (Meyer 1964–67a, 9:11 to 48). During this period they simply put to death whomever they pleased. Then, as their power diminished under Aristobulus II (67–63 B.C.), they reversed their position and opposed the ruling family: First they sent a delegation to Pompey seeking the suppression of the title *king* in their land; then they made the most of Herod the Great's resentment of the nobility. From 4 B.C. to A.D. 66, their political influence waned, but their religious authority waxed apace. They legitimated the current usages and conceptions of popular piety, and this is how they consolidated their authority with the people.

The common people, then, followed the Pharisees. This seemed their only refuge from the influence of the Sadducees—the conservative, hereditary nobility. The people felt closer to the Pharisees than to the aristocracy. The Pharisees, however, by no means considered themselves on the same level with the common people. As their Hebrew name, *Perushim,* indicates, the Pharisees considered themselves "sacred" individuals, people set apart. They were the holy ones, the true Israel.

In spite of their high estimation of themselves and the prestige they enjoyed with the people, the Pharisees were the target of Jesus' scathing criticism. For Jesus their "purity" is impure. It ignores justice and love, and justice and love are the indispensable means of approaching God (Lk 11:39–44). Their devotion to God is of no acccount: what they give God costs them nothing in any way. They recognize God's sovereignty, but only in secondary matters, and not in what would manifest the glory of God more forcefully: relating to others in justice and love (Lk 11:42), mercy and good faith (Mt 23:23). Their pious practices, their fasting, their alms, and their prayer, are not means of approaching God but ways of making use of God (Mt 6:1–6, 16–18).

Jesus' opponents are disturbed and scandalized. The piety of Jesus' disciples is different from that of John's disciples or that of the Pharisees (Mk 2:18). Specifically, concern is expressed that Jesus' disciples are not remarkable for their fasting. Frequent fasting was an important part of Jewish piety. Tacitus bears testimony to this in his writings. For a devout Jew the ideal would be to fast all one's life long (Jdt 8:6). Fasting was held in such high esteem that the *Apocalypse of Elijah* stated that it forgave sins, healed infirmities, drove out evil spirits, and had power before the very throne of God.

Pharisaic moral theology considered fasting superior to alms-giving, as it was done with one's own body, and not merely with money. Fasting was even superior to prayer. The *Jerusalem Talamud* states that one who prays and is not heard should fast (Behm 1964–76, 4:924–36).

Fasting was to the Pharisees a matter of obligation. It had a marked penitential accent. For example, the Pharisees fasted to expiate the apostasy of the people. Fasting was accompanied by a fervent prayer of penitence (Is 58:1–12; 1 Kgs 21:27), grief (1 Sm 31:13), or urgent petition (2 Sm 12:21–23) (Ziesler 1973).

What is at issue here is not the act of fasting but rather what this act of devotion represents. Does it represent a religion of self-interest or one of mournfulness? Jesus' piety breaks with both traditions: It is neither sad nor is it an attempt to place God under an obligation.

Jesus makes no apology for his disciples. He counters with a question of his own. "How can the guests at a wedding fast so long as the groom is still among them?" (Mk 2:19). Taken in isolation, this statement is merely an old saw. But taken in context, it clarifies and reveals the character of Jesus' mission: Jesus bears no resemblance to a person who dotes on sorrow. To be with Jesus, to welcome Jesus, is to be in a situation of gladness that can only be compared with the joy of a wedding-feast. Jesus has not come to weigh people down with precepts; he has come to bestow happiness.

The analogy with the wedding-feast is to be understood on another level as well. Not only is a wedding a time of gladness; it is also a time of salvation (Is 61:10). It is a time of change from oppression to liberation, from discouragement to overflowing gladness (Is 61:1–3). It is a time for the repair of what has been destroyed by oppression (Is 61:3–4). It is a time for the work of the Lord, who loves righteousness and hates iniquity (Is 61:8). The time of the wedding-feast symbolizes the era of God's nearness to and intimacy with his people, the era of the New Jerusalem, the end of the people's lamentation, the time of the manifestation of the liberating activity of the Lord (Is 62:3–4, 5, 7, 11–12).

In the New Testament the wedding is the symbol of the kingdom of God (Mt 25:1–13; Rv 19:7–9)—the kingdom that Jesus announced and proclaimed to be at hand, the kingdom to which all the marginal groups are invited (Lk 14:15–24). This kingdom is the kingdom of gladness and satiety (Mt 22:2–14, along with the other texts cited in this paragraph). Jesus' mission is first and foremost an invitation to joy, the result of God's deed of liberating love in favor of the oppressed people (Mk 2:19). Jesus' behavior and conviviality is an anticipation of the definitive joy of the kingdom.

Jesus' presence is hope and gladness because something has definitively changed. Jesus' time is not one of preparation; hence it is not a time of fasting and penance in the same way that the Baptist's was.

Mark 2:20 is a much disputed verse. Many authors see in it an addition of the primitive church to justify its practice of fasting, and so they consider it a "prophecy after the event" of Jesus' death. This seems rather too facile an explanation, however, for the following reasons. First and foremost, it cannot be ruled out a priori that Jesus foresaw his death. A glance at the recent history of so many Latin Americans who have struggled for social justice will suffice as evidence for that. Second, it is unlikely that the primitive Christian community would have interpolated a prediction of Jesus' death without a prediction of his resurrection.

Jesus did not attack the practice of fasting where his disciples were concerned (Mt 6:16–18). The primitive church, however, was a stranger to any fasting that connoted grief or mourning (Acts 13:2, 14:23). For the primitive church, Jesus was not totally absent. He was present by means of his spirit (Jn 16:7; Acts 1:11). Jesus is with his disciples for all time (Mt 28:20). After the resurrection Jesus awaits them in Galilee (Mk 14:28) (Ziesler 1973).

And so "Jesus replied: 'How can the guests at a wedding fast so long as the groom is still among them? [Mk 2:19a]. So long as the groom stays with them, they cannot fast [19b]. The day will come, however, when the groom will be taken away from them [20a]; on that day they will fast' [20b]." Note the parallelism between verse 19a and 19b. Note further the contrast between verses 19a and 20a, and again between 19b and 20b. This is typical of oral, and Semitic, literature (Taylor 1966, 211).

We must not forget that the material between which these verses are sandwiched, verses 18 and 21–22, underscores the difference between the Pharisees' disciples and Jesus' disciples —not between Jesus' disciples now and Jesus' disciples later (Ziesler 1973). When the Gospel speaks of the disciples' sorrow, of their tribulations (Jn 16:16–23), it is the pangs of childbirth that are being spoken of, the pains of the birth of a new situation for Jesus' disciples. Verses 19a and 20 need not be understood as referring directly to Jesus—as an allegorizing of the person of Jesus—but can refer to those who have, and those who do not have, reasons for rejoicing: to have Jesus produces a burst of joy that nothing can cloud. With Jesus comes joy for the crippled (Mk 2:1-10), for the excluded (2:15-17), for those who decide to follow him (2:13-14, 18, 19). Jesus and his disciples, who make merry and rejoice with the excluded and who show forth the kingdom of God with their way of life and celebration, are very different from those who seek God by rejecting and excluding people. They are even very different from the Baptist.

The Evangelist goes on:

> No one sews a patch of unshrunken cloth on an old cloak. If he should do so, the very thing he has used to cover the hole would pull away—the new from the old—and the tear would get worse. Similarly, no man pours new wine into old wine-skins. If he does so, the wine will burst the skins and both wine and skins will be lost. No, new wine is poured into new skins [Mk 2:21-22].

These verses form an independent unit. They also form a structural and thematic parallel. They are sayings from popular wisdom—old sayings reflecting the usages and experience of poor people. (The rich know nothing of patches on their clothing.) But in context, coming as they do after the two verses immediately preceding, they are an interpretation of Jesus' reply to the question about his praxis.

With these aphorisms drawn from popular wisdom we are shown the incompatibility of the new with the old. Whatever is old lapses, expires, when faced with the new. It is a rule of experience that the new is dangerous for the old. The old is "shown up" by the new; it is overcome by the dynamic power of the new and shows how frail it is by contrast. It offers no resistance. The new triumphs (Hahn 1976, 1:176).

Jesus' words and deeds burst the old order of relationships among human beings. Jesus' friendship, alliance, and involvement with the persons lowest on the social ladder (Mk 2:1-12, 13-14, 15,17) smashes to bits the religious world based on exclusivisms and differences reigning in Palestine.

What Jesus lives, proclaims, and demands cannot be accommodated to this old order. He demonstrates the old order's anti-quated, dilapidated state. By his words, by his hope, and by his life, Jesus is subversive. He does more than call the social order into question. He undermines it, along with the whole religious and mental world in which the majority of human beings, both de facto and necessarily, are looked upon with contempt. Jesus' involve-ment with the physical, social, and religious pariahs of his time irresistibly forces a rupture, a breach, with the old order. Jesus will struggle using every means at his disposal to destroy this order, and its representatives will struggle using their accustomed means to do away with Jesus and with what he represents.

"No, new wine," we hear, "is poured into new skins." The precise meaning of "new skins" is lost in translation here. The Greek word used for "new" in the expression "new skins" is not *neos,* as in the expression "new wine," but—both times it occurs—*kainos*, the same word that is used in the expression "the *new* [pulling away] from the old." That is, the skins are not "new" merely in the sense of being recently made; they are "new" in the sense of replacing what is dilapidated and worn out. The newness spoken of here is a newness not subject to corruption and destruc-tion. It is a newness that is definitive. What is brought to reality with and in Jesus is the newness proclaimed by Second and Third Isaiah. It is the novelty of the Lord's triumph, which will be made manifest in the healing of the sick and the liberation of the op-pressed (Is 43:7, 9–10). It is the materialization of the Lord's deed of justice (Is 43:19–20, 41:20).

Jesus' novelty, Jesus' newness, is the new creation announced by Third Isaiah (Is 65:17). It is the joy of the people and the joy of God with the people. It is the people transformed into gladness (Is 65:18–19). It is the complete transformation of this world, the eradication of every kind of exploitation (Is 65:21–22). It is the end of the situation denounced by the prophets, the abolition of the situation in which poor persons are hemmed in on all sides and cannot enjoy the fruits of their own labor. It is the contrary of the lot decreed for the exploiters (Am 5:11), the fraudulent, and the rich, who are full of violence (Mi 6:6–16) (Muilenberg 1951–57, 5:753). It is the triumph of peace, in which no persons impose their wills on others (Is 65:24–25). This is the sort of message and praxis we have with Jesus. This is the novelty of Jesus, shown in his teaching (Mk 1:27) and his deeds (2:21–22), which prepares us to drink a new wine (Mk 14:25) in a world transformed—a world of corporeal transformation issuing in perfect communion with God (Jeremias 1966, 218).

THE SACRED RIGHT OF THE POOR

The observance of the sabbath was one of the mainstays of religious life in the Palestine of Jesus' day. It has its origins in the earliest history of Yahwism (de Vaux 1967, 377). The sanctity of the sabbath derives from its relationship with the God of the Covenant and from its status as a part of that Covenant. It is a tithe of time—one day in the week consecrated to Yahweh—and it is referred to in the various formulations of the Covenant (deVaux 1967, 378).

Besides its character as something consecrated to the Lord, the sabbath also has a social aspect and a special place in salvation history:

> For six days you may do your work, but on the seventh day you must rest, that your ox and your ass may also have rest, and that the son of your maidservant and the alien may also be refreshed [Ex 23:12].

> For remember that you too were once slaves in Egypt, and the Lord, your God, brought you from there with his strong hand and outstretched arm. That is why the Lord, your God, has commanded you to observe the sabbath day [Dt 5:15].

Rigorism with regard to the observance of the sabbath began only after the Exile. Prescriptions concerning the sabbath became so strict that the *Book of Jubilees* forbids marriage, the kindling of a fire, and the preparation of food on the sabbath.

In post-Exilic Judaism the sabbath is the sign of the divine election. Three tractates of the *Mishnah* (*Shabbat, Erubin,* and *Beza*) treat exclusively of the sabbath. The Second Book of Maccabees considers the celebration of the sabbath one of the principal characteristics of being a Jew (6.6).

Rabbinical theology was sure that "if Israel would observe but two sabbaths as it is prescribed, the day of redemption would come." Thus wrote Rabbis Shimon ben Yojai around A.D. 150 (*Babylonia Talmud*, Shabbat 118). The sabbath has more weight than all the other commandments of the Law together (*Jerusalem Talmud*, Berakhot 1). The celebration of the sabbath is an anticipation of eternal glory (*Jubilees* 2:19, 21; 50:9). Therefore the one who toils on the sabbath merits death (*Jubilees* 2:19) as one who has profaned that sabbath (Lohse 1964-76, 7:1-34). Strict observance of the sabbath was a sign of earnestness and reverence in the sight of God. It was a sign of the renunciation of carelessness and levity.

The Pharisees mitigated the sabbatical rigorism demanded by other religious groups. They observed the sabbath with some regard for practical circumstances and took care not to destroy the sabbath joy. Accordingly, rabbis permitted toil on the sabbath such as was necessary to save someone's life. The *Mishâna* only prohibited doing thirty-nine kinds of work (plus their subdivisions) on the sabbath.

Jesus and his disciples were poor. They had no one to prepare their sabbath meal a day in advance, nor the wherewithal to preserve it if it were prepared. And so it happened that one day as they were walking through some fields, they plucked some spikes of grain to eat as they went along their way (Mk 2:23)—a twofold violation of the sabbath. The Pharisees did not lose the opportunity of remarking that Jesus took no action against the illicit practice of his disciples. "Look!" say the Pharisees (In Greek, *ide*, "look," "behold"—used here in the sense of "just imagine!" [Mk 2:24b]. The discovery is a serious one. The accusation could have brought Jesus death by stoning.

Jesus' reply is scarcely a learned one. Even his reference to a high priest in the time of David is anachronistic (Benoit 1968, 3/1:223). Further, 1 Samuel 21:2 mentions an Ahimelech, not an Abiathar. What is important is that Jesus opposes his own reading of scripture, the reading of a poor person, to the reading of the Pharisees, the reading of the influential. The point is to determine whom or what the Law is designed to serve (Mk 2:25-26). Jesus challenges the Pharisees to read the story of David's flight in 1 Samuel 21 from a different perspective. "Have you never read what David did when he was in need and he and his men were hungry? How he entered God's house in the days of Abiathar the high priest and ate the holy bread which only the priests were permitted to eat? He even gave it to his men" (Mk 2:25–26). In other words, Jesus is telling them that it is he who is of the line of David, not they. He understands and lives the Law as David did. David placed consecrated bread at the service of a group of hungry and needy persons. Jesus is placing the sabbath at the service of poor and hungry persons.

For Jesus the most sacred thing that exists is the alleviation of the needs of the poor. Before all else, the sabbath is at the service of the needy (Mk 2:27). For Jesus the reason for which the sabbath was instituted by God—*egeneto* in the original, "was made," a word reminiscent of the first creation—was the human being, the human being who is suffering hunger and affliction (2:27a). Jesus relates the Law to God, and accordingly posits it as a help, a service, to the poor, as indeed this particular law was intended originally: an expression of the sacred nature of the right of the poor to take their rest.

Pierre Benoit advances a very middle-class reason for doubting the authenticity of Mark 2:27 as Jesus' own words. He writes that Jesus' statement "relativizes the sabbath obligation, subordinating it to welfare, and to the welfare of any human being. Such an attitude would have been most surprising in the time and circumstances of the Gospel" (Benoit 1968, 3/1:233). And of course Jesus did cause great *astonishment*. Otherwise he would not have had enemies. Was this not precisely the cause of Jesus' death and the reason for such conflict during his ministry? He is not softening the strictness of the Law; he is placing the whole of the Law in the service of a few poor persons. He is not even subordinating the sabbath observance to human beings in general. He is subordinating it to the human being who is hungry and in need. Clearly Jesus' statement is a challenge to the whole of Judaic legislation. For Jesus nothing, not even the most sacred law, may be allowed to obstruct the liberation of the human being. It is the human being who is more worthy of respect and reverence. Here lies the root of Jesus' conflict with the authorities and intellectuals of his time. Because of his respect for the human being, not because of any sacristy disputes, Jesus' enemies contrive his death.

Verse 27, then, is an authentic commentary and an authentic justification of Jesus' practice.

The connective, "That is why" (v. 28—*hōste* in the original Greek), just as in Mark 10:11, links what follows not only with the preceding verse but with the whole preceding scene. It has the same scope and substance as Mark 2:10: "That you may know that the Son of Man has authority on earth to forgive sins. . . . " The whole episode manifests the Son of Man as lord of the sabbath (Minette de Tillesse 1968, 128–43).

By relating this verse to the preceding scene, Jesus makes it clear that he sees his lordship (2:28) as being in the service of all the oppressed. Jesus has received the power to inaugurate a new era— an era of pardon and definitive joy—and to annihilate all chains (to paraphrase and reinterpret Minette de Tillesse). The exercise of his power places Jesus at odds with the lords of this world. Confronted with Jesus' lordship, legalism becomes helpless. After all, it too was originally intended for the benefit of oppressed human beings.

UNDER SURVEILLANCE

From menacing protest (Mk 2:24) the Pharisees move to surveillance (3:2), and from surveillance to the decision, taken jointly with the Herodians, to kill Jesus (3:6). The authorization Jesus gives his disciples to violate the sabbath (2:25) sparks the surveillance. Its purpose is to see whether Jesus may be caught at something deserving of capital punishment, as prescribed in the Pentateuch: "You must keep the sabbath as something sacred. Whoever desecrates it shall be put to death. . . . [such a one] must be rooted out of his people" (Ex 31:14).

The Pharisees have no interest in the person with the withered hand (Mk 3), nor, certainly, in any remedy for his suffering. Their sole interest is in the faults that might be being committed by the one who will attempt to deliver him from his misfortune and from evil.

The Pharisees were on the watch (Mk 3:2). They were spying. And yet Jesus was performing his works in broad daylight (3:3–5). Jesus' adversaries made use of the Law to blind themselves to other people's suffering (3:5) and to do away with creative, liberating life (3:6).

Jesus' attitude is provocative. He takes the initiative. He calls to the person with the withered hand. He orders him to stand up in the view of all (3:3). There is no need for the sufferer to speak to Jesus and still less for him to humble himself. The sufficient, and more than sufficient, argument in favor of an attempt to cure him is his suffering. The cure could have been performed on some other day, of course. The patient was not in danger of death. He did not have to be healed on the sabbath. But there is more at stake here than a prodigious power of healing.

Jesus provokes his adversaries with a question. "Is it permitted to do a good deed on the sabbath—or an evil one? To preserve life—or to destroy it?" (Mk 3:4). There is a great deal behind Jesus' double question. What Jesus calls a "good deed" here is the suppression of what diminishes or wastes a human being. Jesus relates the will of God to the material, corporeal salvation of human beings. Jesus asks whether God is manifested in healing or in not healing, in suppressing suffering or in leaving human beings in their suffering—in saving someone from incipient death or in spying on a person in order to kill him (Taylor 1966, 222). Jesus is inviting his adversaries to question themselves and to answer whether God is on the side of oppression and tyranny or on that of succor and life. He is challenging them to say whether God is revealed in death or in life. Jesus' practice leads to life; his adversaries' practice leads to death. True Law—the true manifestation of God's will—is that observed by Jesus.

Jesus not only reduces legalism to the absurd, he also uncovers what lurks behind a bare, sterile, aggressive orthodoxy. In the confrontation Jesus is pointing to the root of his freedom and to the root of the opposition he is encountering. His adversaries are prisoners of law and of nearsighted interpretations of law. Their imprisonment grows out of their attachment to compromises, prejudices, and privileges. Jesus is free, for his attachment is to those who suffer material privation.

The Pharisees make no reply. Faced with the real questions, faced with what really concerns the majority of people, they have not a word to say. They are mute (Mk 9:34), for they are afraid to bring out into the open what they really seek. And they persevere in their intent to indict Jesus and to annihilate him (Mk 3:6).

As the Pharisees fall silent Jesus looks in anger and sorrow at them with their "closed minds" (literally, "their hardness of heart") and decides to go ahead with the cure (Mk 3:5). Jesus is angry and sorrowful, over the Pharisees' attachment to dead formularies, over a blindness toward the liberating will of God being made manifest in his praxis (Mk 6:52, 8:17).

Jesus is impatient with those who—in the name of God—refuse to allow the liberation of wasted bodies, with those who are opposed—for religious motives—to the suppression of exclusivism and contempt for people. Jesus expresses his anger by rebuking the attitude of indifference his adversaries are taking toward a situation of suffering. The same passion led him to drive the merchants—those who identified God with exclusivism and mercantilism (Mk 11:15-19)—from the temple. God entertains the same anger toward those who refuse to accept the messianic message of gladness (Lk 14:21), toward those who refuse to bestow on others what they have freely received from God themselves (Mt 18:34). Jesus reveals the true will of God. He heals on the sabbath in order to demonstrate that nothing can separate God's cause from the struggle against the suffering of poor and marginalized human beings. By opposing Jesus' praxis, his adversaries, the Law's official defenders, have denied God, who is the cause and purpose of the Law. This denial is the "hardness of heart" spoken of in the Deuteronomic tradition.

Incapable of struggling against the physical, material suffering of others, the Pharisees are unable to accept God's will. Hence they plot to rid themselves of Jesus. The divine will is getting too close for comfort. As they are adamantly opposed to the revelation of God's subversive, liberating love, nothing remains for them but to murder Jesus. To achieve this end, they ally themselves with the Herodians (Mk 3:6). Legalism and religious purism now join with political opportunism, the denial of morality in politics, hunger for power, crass impiety, and tyranny.

PARALLELS IN LUKE'S GOSPEL

Two other events, which only the Gospel of Luke relates, are like the event reported in Mark 3:1-6 and can shed more light on Jesus' mentality.

The Human Being as above All Law

In the synagogue one sabbath Jesus encounters a woman who had had to go about doubled over for eighteen years, without ever being able to hold her head up. Jesus takes the initiative. He calls the afflicted woman to him and says, "You are free of your infirmity" (Lk 13:12). The chief of the synagogue is scandalized. He is not concerned for the crippled woman; he is concerned for the sabbath (13:14).

Jesus calls this concern hypocrisy (13:15). Rabbinical moral theology permitted untying an ox or an ass on the sabbath to lead it to drink. The rabbis saw no incompatibility between the observance of the sabbath and the safeguarding of their legitimate interests, but they did see Jesus' liberation of this woman from the bonds of her infirmity as incompatible with the honor due God (13:15–16). For Jesus, the woman is religiously incomplete. She is "in the bondage of Satan" (13:16). And yet she is a daughter of Abraham, an heiress of the Promise!

What matters to Jesus is this person. What matters to the chief of the synagogue is the observance of a law. Jesus speaks of bondage and release (13:16). Untying a knot was one of the classic forbidden activities, but even here there was a way out of the prohibition: Rabbi Meir (ca. 150 B.C.) wrote that a knot that could be undone with one hand could be undone on the sabbath. Yet our legalists will not apply this leniency in favor of relief for a body in misery.

Once more Jesus rescues the best in tradition and restores it to life. For Jesus any person is worth more than property. For him this crippled woman, useless to society, is superior in value and dignity to any means of gain whatsoever. He cites the Pharisees' attitude toward human suffering as an example of their impenitence (cf. Lk 13:1–9).

Abolition of All Manner of Discrimination

Parallel to this pericope is Luke 14:1–5. The content is the same as far as Jesus' discussion with the Pharisees is concerned. What lends the Lukan pericope deeper significance is the context. Jesus has been invited to a banquet (Lk 14:1). He takes advantage of the occasion to speak of the conditions for true conviviality: not to exalt oneself (14:7–11) and a disinterestedness, an altruism of the highest order, with regard to sharing one's joy (14:12–14). Then Jesus speaks of the banquet of the kingdom, of the messianic joy that the rich reject and the destitute accept (14:15–24). Finally, he warns that in order to live this joy one must sacrifice everything else (14:25–33).

Dropsy, in the rabbinical opinion, was caused by the sin of lust (Strack and Billerbeck 1922–28, 203). Jesus does not succeed in communicating with the leading Pharisee who has invited him to dinner or with the other invited guests. He speaks to them, but he rejects the sort of unity and joy that they defend. What interests Jesus is the liberation of bodies and consciences. This, he says, will produce joy without end.

His audience does not speak. They are too busy spying (Lk 14:1). They have need of the dark (cf. Lk 22:53). It is Jesus who speaks (Lk 14:2–5). Faced with a new order in which discrimination, prejudice, and class prerogatives are to be abolished, the pharisaic moral theology is mute (Lk 14:6). Unlike the great ones among his people, Jesus has not come to be an additional burden for those who have nothing. He has come as their rescuer and their gladness.

Chapter 2

Jesus' Power and Strength

MIRACLES

When we speak of miracles, a smile of superiority is likely to come to our lips. The miracle fever the "gringo" sects use to distract us from our vital problems—our living problems—have contributed to our loss of a true sense of miracle. Our ideas and beliefs about Jesus' miracles are confused. We refuse to look on Jesus as a kind of religious showman. We prefer the seriousness and authenticity of the human drama right here on earth: we have no need of the heavenly variety, we feel. And so we lightly rationalize the gospel accounts of Jesus' miracles, lest we lose track of the seriousness of the gospel. Or perhaps we are afraid of falling victim to the idea-manipulators. Or, worst of all, perhaps we are afraid of being too much like the ignorant masses of the poor.

Before we accept or reject the fact of a miracle, we ought to reflect upon the meaning of miracle as such. Certain gospel narratives of the miracles of Jesus will be of help to us here.

God's Language for Everybody

God is revealed through deeds and events. In them God's revealing word is addressed to human beings. The material universe is not mere decoration. Nor is it a mirage. No, it is the indispensable means of interpersonal communication. God speaks to us in the language of matter. God, who intervenes in my consciousness, also

28

speaks to my bodily reality, for there is no thought process without its immediate corporeal correlate, no thinking of any sort without the direct participation of the body in that act of thinking (Mouroux 1953, 47).

As Pascal said, we need both truth and miracles, for it is the whole human being who has to be convinced, body as well as soul (Pascal 1962, 806). To deny miracles would be to reduce God to the status of a part of our inner selves. It would be to divorce human beings from their nature and to deny matter any future. By means of miracles God refuses to be the monopoly of the know-it-alls. He speaks everybody's language (Jn 7:31–52).

Through the incarnation God somehow descends to this material organism of ours and is steeped in our need and our toil and our pain until God is actually brought down to destruction and death. After that occurs our bodies can be drawn to God (Mouroux 1953, 75). Jesus is the manifestation of the glory of God. He cannot be reduced to an idea, not even the most sublime idea. Redemption is effectuated in and for this material world. Jesus shows any interest in a disincarnate world. The glory of the Lord cannot be walled up in the world of ideas. The gospel is not intellectual, nor are mystical happenings reserved for the initiate. They are materialistic in the best sense of the word. Jesus does not reveal himself as immortality and thought, but as resurrection and life (Jn 11:25).

Signs of Liberation

Jesus' preaching is a call to conversion, a summons to accept God's triumph. It cannot be separated from deliverance from bodily slaveries (Lk 4:17–21). Jesus commits all his strength against the murderous might that enslaves people's bodies (Lk 13:16; Jn 8:44). With Jesus the future is present here and now. The "new heaven," where justice reigns, has already come. Jesus' activity is the anticipation of future total victory over the power of destruction and death.

Jesus has a body. He reveals himself to us in and through that body. In him it is revealed to us that the Resurrection is God's last word, and that our own body, which is one day to rise again—strong, filled with the Spirit, glorious, and incorruptible

(1 Cor 15:43–44)—can taste the bountiful power of God even today.

The Christian miracle is disconcerting, unsettling. It is a summons to consciences (Mt 11:20–21). It places our self-centered securities and aspirations in abeyance—in the multiplication of the loaves (Lk 6:30–44), for example, money ceases to be motive and goal of one's activities and desires.

When he works a miracle, Jesus never displays the arrogance of the rich. In every detail his power is the contrary of the power of the oppressor. Jesus never forces himself on people—neither by threats nor by propaganda—as do the rich. Jesus refuses to perform a miracle that would only serve his own good or that would lend itself to sensationalism: either he imposes silence or he works his miracle far from people's view (Mk 1:44, 5:43, 7:36, 8:26). Hence he does not even perform miracles before his own compatriots, who are scandalized at his poverty (Mk 6:1–6). Nor does he work any miracles during his Passion.

The earmark of the Christian miracle is not that it is a prodigy but rather that it is an anticipation of the human being's deliverance from all harm. It is a challenge to conscience. It is an incitement to faith. This is the important thing. This is why the true miracle does not please everyone: we have but to recall the cure of the person born blind (Jn 9), the raising of Lazarus (Jn 11), and the miracles Jesus worked on the sabbath (Mk 3:1–6; Lk 13:10–17, 14:1–6; Jn 5:1–18). In each case someone reacted hostilely to the miracle. Hence, in the Old Testament, miracles are called signs. In the first three Gospels they are called *dunámeis*, "acts of power," for they are the product of the dynamic force that lives in Jesus. They speak to us of the power and life that have come with Jesus. They are "words" proclaiming the kingdom, words containing Jesus' message (Leon-Dufour 1964). As Augustine put it, "The deeds of the Word, too, are words for us" (*Commentary on John,* 24:6). Concretely, in Mark's Gospel the wonderful works of Jesus in favor of the sick are "gospel"—the good news of the kingdom—and this is why the sick need no other prerequisite than to be in misery and dereliction (Kertelge 1970, 38).

The essence of Jesus' miracles lies not in their stupendousness and verifiability but in their reference to the person of Jesus. They manifest his nearness to God, his triumph over the powers that destroy the human being, and the might of his limitless love as it is revealed to us in his Resurrection.

The miracles have relevance for us because they reveal to us what Jesus is. In other words they have meaning for us because Jesus has meaning for us (Kertelge 1970, 207).

Good News for the Downtrodden

Mark 1:40–45 tells us of the healing of a leper. Here we can see the marvelous power of Jesus. Leprosy was considered a fatal disease (2 Kgs 7:3, 15:5). It was called the "first-born of death" (Jb 18:13) and was looked upon as the worst form of bodily impurity that could infect a human being (von Rad 1967, 1:241). The *Babylonian Talmud* names four classes of people to be considered as good as dead: the poor, the blind, the sterile, and lepers.

Lepers had to keep away from the community. They had to live apart, "with their own kind," as they were ritually unclean and thus threatened the purity of the people. "The one who bears the sore of leprosy shall keep his garments rent and his head bare, and shall muffle his beard; he shall cry out, 'Unclean, unclean!' As long as the sore is on him he shall declare himself unclean, since he is in fact unclean. He shall dwell apart, making his abode outside the camp" (Lv 13:45–46).

Lepers were prohibited from entering Jerusalem or any of the old walled cities. In the cities where they were admitted, special precautions were taken against them because whatever they might touch became impure. Lepers were stigmatized as persons who had been struck down by the wrath of God (Nm 12:10–15; Kgs 5:19–27). Leprosy was even called the "stroke," the "blow" (Eichrodt 1961–67, 1:135). The affliction was considered divine punishment for slander, pride, or murder (Grundmann 1962, 52–53). Touching a leper rendered one incapable of offering worship to God (Strack and Billerbeck 1922–28, 4/2: 751–53). This will explain the phobia of Rabbi Resh Lakish, who stoned lepers whenever he saw them. It will also explain the fastidiousness of certain other rabbis. Some, for instance, refused to eat eggs from hens that had been allowed to roam in an alley where a leper lived.

Any society concerned for its preservation has commands and prohibitions by which it seeks to forestall its own dissolution and death. For the people of Israel, God was life, and the greatest obstacle to approaching him was death. According to tradition the closest thing to death was leprosy. The leaders in Israel vigorously decried the violence that was caused by disease or by anything that looked like death. But they closed their eyes to the violence caused by human relationships. As a result they easily fell into abstractions, and their religious thought was de facto a justification of the currently prevailing social situation.

The leper who approaches Jesus expresses limitless confidence in him. "If you will to do so," he cries, "you can cure me." And Jesus answers, "I do will it. Be cured" (Mk 1:41). This is not just a cure; it is a purification. The man can no longer be excluded; he can no longer be regarded as an enemy of God and a danger to society. The word Mark uses (v. 44), which is translated as "cure" ("Offer for your cure what Moses prescribed," Jesus tells the man) is *katharismós*, literally, "purification." The noun and its cognate verb *katharizō*, in both Jewish law and the gospels (see also Lk 2:22; Jn 2:6), connote the reestablishment of cultic purity (Hauck 1964–76a, 3:41–26).

Jesus allows this leper, this worst of all social outcasts, physically to approach him! Jesus even touches him (Mk 1:41). Jesus is not afraid of soiling himself. This is not the kind of impurity he attacks. The impurity he attacks is the one that brings on real death, the one that endangers one's nearness to God.

Jesus is able to look beyond the loathesomeness and devastation caused by this terrible disease. He is able to see the suffering of a concrete human being. This intense compassion, this total solidarity with the outcast and the suffering, merited Jesus exclusion from respectable Jewish society (Taylor 1966, 187). With Jesus the barriers society has constructed within itself collapse. Jesus is interested in something more than a particular society's self-preservation. He is interested in the suppression of human humiliation. Wherever Jesus is, all reason for segregation disappears. No more may suffering human beings be branded as abominable. Jesus' radical repugnance for evil creates genuine purity.

Jesus is not emotionally impassive or stoical in the face of the leper's painful situation. He is "moved with pity" (Mk 1:41). Then he heals the leper with his word. The healing of a leper was considered something only God could do (2 Kgs 5:7). Healing a leper, in the Jewish mind, was as difficult as raising someone from the dead (Kertelge 1970, 66). Jesus behaves like a new Elisha (2 Kgs 5:8–19), but with an important difference: he allows the leper to approach him, to touch him. And the touch restores the sick man to purity.

For the people of the biblical age, one of the characteristics of the "last days"—one of the earmarks of the "end-time," the moment of the definitive manifestation of peace and welfare—was to be the healing of lepers (Mt 11:5; Lk 7:2). Jesus acts as God; he acts with divine power (Kertelge 1979, 66). He is the long-awaited prophet (Jn 6:14, 7:40). In him all the salvific power of God is made manifest.

During Jesus' lifetime on earth, and for a generation or so after, there arose in Palestine a series of rebel leaders who claimed to be the vessels, the bearers, of the promised, longed-for salvation. A certain Theudas, who is mentioned in Acts 5:36, claimed to be the new Joshua who would snatch Jerusalem and the temple out of the hands of the Romans. A Samaritan in the time of Pontius Pilate showed his followers objects taken from the temple and buried, according to Samaritan tradition, on Mount Gerizim: in other words, he proclaimed he was the new Moses. During the administration of the procurator Felix, an Egyptian incited "four thousand cutthroats" to riot (Acts 21:38), hoping to do to Jerusalem what Joshua had done to Jericho. Jonathan of Cyrene, a *Sicarius* (a violent Jewish nationalist), enticed poor Jews from Pentapolis, in Libya, into the desert with the promise of miracles and visions (Meyer 1964–76b, 6:78–861). All these rebels provoked in the people a desire to throw off the yoke of oppression and domination. But the only result was repression and death. Jesus' power was different. Jesus' power was manifested in his oneness with outcasts and in his efforts to restore them to social acceptance.

Jesus orders the leper to show himself to the priests that this "should be a proof for them" (Mk 1:44)—*eis marturion autois,* that is, in fulfillment of a formal legal obligation (Mk 6:11, 13:9; Jas 5:3). Now the leper's cure would stand as a living accusation against spiritual leaders who, despite Jesus' miraculous cures, failed to see in him the advent of the liberating power of God (Is 35:5).

Signs of an Abundance of Love

The account of the multiplication of the loaves (Mk 6:30–44) continues to be the butt of the humor of the pseudointelligentsia down to our own day. In Jesus' time the miracle aroused the fury of those who saw in it—as indeed in prayer—a magical rite with an automatic effect. Both attitudes are obstacles to a correct understanding of the event.

The account of this miracle leaves several things unexplained: first how five thousand people could gather in a region of the country where the largest "city" surely had a population of no more than three thousand; second, how so many people could have decided all at once that they knew where to find Jesus and must go out to see him; third, how such large numbers of people did not attract the attention of Jesus' enemies.

Further, it was well into the evening when the miracle was performed. Now, it must have taken some time to divide the crowd into groups of fifty or a hundred. It must have taken still more time to distribute the bread among so many people. Finally, the disciples would have had to collect what was left—filling twelve baskets. This must have taken more time. What about having to carry those twelve baskets of food through the deserted countryside afterwards? How difficult, not to say meaningless, this would have been. And where did the disciples go for the containers in the first place? To the towns round about? Why did they not simply go to those towns for food? Finally, what eventually became of these twelve baskets of food? These puzzles indicate to us that the evangelist is not seeking to communicate a detailed chronicle of an event. Rather he is attempting to reveal to us something that will be of value to us. The concern here is not a knowledge of past events but an experience of faith. This is the story of a mystery, and so it calls for an understanding that goes deeper than apparent "facts" (Dodd 1976, 200).

The reason Jesus performed this miracle for the people is altogether clear in the Gospel of Mark: "He pitied them, for they were like sheep without a shepherd . . ." (6:34). "To pity" fails to express the whole meaning of the verb *splangchnisthomai*. Except in the parables, the subject of this verb in the Gospels is never anyone but Jesus himself. It is the equivalent of the verb *makrothumeo,* "to behave with high-mindedness," or "to persevere in understanding," corresponding to the English word "long-suffering." It is the contrary of "to go into a rage" (*orkizomai*). These expressions are among the strongest the Greek language has to show human emotions.

Splangchnisthomai is strikingly reminiscent of "emotions of God" in the Old Testament and hence connotes the divine element in Jesus' action. It indicates that God's own mercy is being exercised here (Köster 1964–76, 7:548–59). Jesus' emotion is aroused by the plight of the people—these "sheep without a shepherd." He reacts interiorly to their state of dereliction and abandonment. A "flock," of course, calls up a familiar Old Testament image of the people of God (see, for example, Ps 77:21; Jer 23:1; Ez 43:10, 55).

The expression "sheep without a shepherd" appears in Numbers 27:17 and Ezekiel 34:8. Mark's account is influenced by Psalm 23:

> The Lord is my *shepherd;* I shall *not want.*
> In verdant *pastures* he gives me *repose*;
> Beside restful waters he leads me . . . [v 1].

"Restful waters" is *hydatos anapauseōs,* and Mark's *anapausasthe oligon,* "[come] . . . rest a little," recalls this expression. "He began to teach them" (Mk 6:34) may recall verse 3 of the psalm, "He guides me in right paths" (Schürmann 1969, 513).

The figure of the Lord as a shepherd, of the Messiah as shepherd of the people, is not rare in the Old Testament, and of course the Old Testament was rooted in the whole cultural matrix of the Middle East. Gathering his scattered people, governing with justice, and caring for the weak constitute the pastoral function of the ideal sovereign (Jeremias 1964–76b, 6:485–99).

In the psalms, the Lord appears as shepherd of the people of Israel, guiding them along the paths of liberation and rescuing them from Pharaoh's repression (Ps 77:20–21, 78:52). They, having reached the utmost depths of oppression (Ps 79:1–14) and believing that their helplessness is complete (79:8), ask the Lord, their shepherd, to deliver them from their sins (v 9), from oppression, from murder, and from humiliation (vv 10–12). The

Lord, reminded of having led the people from slavery to freedom, now is asked to deliver them from suffering, ridicule, and humiliation (Ps 80:1-8).

Psalm 23, which seems to have exerted such influence on the narrative of the multiplication of the loaves in Mark 6, expresses boundless confidence in the Lord, for in the Lord the people find refuge in the face of the enemy. They experience a special security and tranquility at the hands of the divine goodness.

Jeremiah pronounces judgment on the shepherds who scatter the Lord's sheep and lead them astray (Jer 23:1-2). They are Israel's evil leaders, and the sheep no one cares for are the people (Rudolph 1968, 145). This situation is destined to be remedied: God promises the people that fear and destruction will come to an end, thanks to the shepherds he will give them (Jer 23:4). The ideal king will be just the opposite of the shepherds the people now have. Through him, the people will enjoy the peace that is born of right and justice (23:5-6).

In a great oracle of the restoration of Israel (31:10-14), Jeremiah proclaims that the Lord will gather the people together and keep them once more, as a shepherd gathers and guards his flock. The Lord's shepherding consists in snatching the people of Israel from the power of an enemy more powerful than they, and in leading them to a place of freedom and abundance where there is no hunger and where all have everything they need (Rudolph 1968, 196). How the people rejoice, now that all their distress is ended!

Ezekiel, in the prophecies he utters against the shepherds of Israel, speaks of leaders who have been profiteers and exploiters, exposing the people to all manner of calamities (Ez 34:1-10). The image is one of injustice and violence afflicting a people in misery. The prophecy is a protest against the political leaders of Israel (Eichrodt 1966, 327). The crime being denounced is a social one (329). In the face of this situation, the Lord promises to come and be the people's shepherd. The Lord will rule to the advantage of the weak and the dispossessed (Ez 34:14), delivering them from the cruelty of their leaders (v 10) so that the dominant sectors will cease their abuse and exploitation (vv 21-22). When the Lord at last shepherds the flock, the situation of oppression will be done away with (v 23).

In the Book of the Consolation of Israel (Is 40–66), the prophet proclaims the end of the people's servitude, the inauguration of an era like that of their deliverance from the power of Pharaoh, and the imminent coming of the Lord. Then shall the Lord be as a shepherd to the people (Is 40:11). In other words, God will care for the weak and the needy.

The *Damascus Document* (13:9), in its discussion of the duties of the *Mebaqqer,* the leader of the community who has been entrusted with the care of the people, states:

> He must be merciful, as a father toward his sons . . . and as a shepherd he must unshackle them from all the shackles with which they have been shackled.

In the rabbinic era the masters of the Law were called shepherds. But Mark's outlook is closer to the Old Testament than it is to rabbinism.

In providing the poor with their miraculous meal, Jesus shows himself to be their shepherd, their liberator, the answer to the needs of a people in danger of collapse. In the banquet that Jesus spreads, all dine in abundance, all dine on the same food, and all receive the same attention. It is a meal for all, and the poor have been invited. Jesus celebrates and dines with the outcast so as to fill them with joy (Mk 2:15–17). Without self-interest, he provides a hungry, scourged people with nourishment. It is the feast-day of the poor. With Jesus near, the poor are on holiday. With Jesus, you don't need money. The divine mercy, not money, meets the needs and hopes of an exploited people. In Jesus are fulfilled the hopes of a people whom the Lord means to rescue from every slavery. Jesus takes the needs of the people to heart. In Jesus, God's power is present in total commitment to the oppressed. It is God who is Jesus' driving force, and thus it is God who is the people's shepherd.

It would be an easy matter to reduce the pastoral function of Jesus to teaching, especially if we were to argue that in rabbinism the masters of the Law were called shepherds, and that, according to Mark's text, after Jesus' attitude of pity for the people has been set forth, "he began to teach them at great length" (Mk 6:34). The pastoral consequences of this interpretation, it seems to me, would be disastrous. In addition to what has already been said on this point, let me cite a beautiful passage by Karl Kertelge:

That day at Capernaum, there is no discourse for us to read, even though we have read in Mark 1:21 that he has taught in the synagogue. Instead, it is related to us in great detail how he cured a possessed person in that synagogue (1:23–28), that he healed Peter's mother-in-law (1:29–31), and that he went on healing after that (1:32–34). This bestows a special meaning on the exclamation of the astonished witnesses of the expulsion of the demon in the synagogue: "What does this mean? A completely new teaching in a spirit of authority!" (1:27). The people are praising a new way of teaching, an authoritative way of teaching, and they make no reference to the preceding discourse. Rather they refer to Jesus' actions. The relationship between the *euangellion,* then, the Good News, and the marvelous works of Jesus is straightforwardly available in the familiar formula "words and works." In Mark, both are interlaced. Jesus' marvelous deeds *are* his Gospel [Kertelge 1970, 38].

Let us remember that the miracle of the Christ, the Messiah, is only an anticipation of the definitive manifestations of the power of God's goodness. Its function is to reveal God's project to us, and to encourage and accompany us along the path of its accomplishment.

Signs in the Community

The account of the multiplication of the loaves bears a great similarity to Exodus 16, not because of the desert theme—since Mark's *erēmos topos* is not a "desert" but simply an unsettled region—but by reason of the pressing physical needs of the people and the solution that they find.

In the desert of the Sinai, the people are on the point of dying of hunger (Ex 16:3). They have suffered under the yoke of slavery and are on their way to freedom. The remedy for their hunger, the reason they do not fail in midcourse, is the bread the Lord gives them (16:16). They are satisfied, for they eat manna in abundance (16:13), a quarter of a peck apiece (16:16)—an astonishing amount, enough for an entire family. The food cannot be stored, however. It is vain to speculate on the gifts of the Lord (16:6–10), the gifts that are the Lord's response to the needs of the people.

A related account in Numbers 11 tells of the crowds who are hungering (11:4) and of Moses, who sees no possibility of alleviating their need (v 21). Then the Lord is told of the crisis (v 13), just as the disciples tell Jesus of the people's need (Mk 6:35, and especially 8:4)—whereupon all receive an abundant supply of quail (Nm 11:32), and the word of the Lord is accomplished. The people see that it is God's power that has wrought all this (Nm 11:23). Anyone eating more than need dictates, however, dies the death (11:31–35).

What God has done in the Old Testament for the people is realized in a supereminent, definitive manner with Jesus. And here we see the good sense of certain "incongruities." Our account tells us of five thousand people who join Jesus in a wild, lonely district. The purpose of the account is to give us to understand that Jesus is help for and response to the needs of the deceived, wrung-out multitudes. In Jesus' deeds we are shown the meaning of the power of God. What the wretched masses have hoped for from God is now given to us in Jesus.

Signs of Service and of Relationship with the Father

There are a good many structural correspondences between Mark 6:30–46 and 2 Kings 4:42–44. The two prodigies related are both miracles of multiplication. But there are differences as well. Jesus does not have servants; he has disciples. The disproportion between the provisions on hand and the people to be fed is much greater in Jesus' case. Jesus feeds the hungering masses of common, ordinary people. In the gospel account there is no direct reference to the word of the Lord, as there is in 2 Kings 4:43: Jesus is not simply a spokesperson proclaiming a wonder to be worked by the Lord; he and the Father are acting in concert (Kertelge 1970, 517).

The present account also differs from the account of the institution of the Eucharist. Here it is the disciples who distribute the loaves. They wait upon the crowd as they will wait upon the community at table one day in the future (Acts 6:2). They give food to the hungry throng as they will later distribute the Eucharist and nourishment to those in need (Acts 2:42–47, 4:32–37). This is the function of a disciple: to be at Jesus' service as he seeks to satisfy all the hunger of his people.

With Jesus the superabundance of the messianic times is upon us. In him the power of God's goodness is rendered present. Jesus' deeds prefigure the definitive realization of the hopes of the oppressed, the fulfillment of the divine promises. But then as now, the disciples did not understand Jesus.

"They gathered up enough leftovers to fill twelve baskets, besides what remained of the fish" (Mk 6:43). Here is another of the "happy incongruities." The number of baskets remaining was twelve. Just as we do not know where the disciples obtained the baskets, neither do we know how they disposed of them. But we do know that Jesus had twelve apostles. Clearly the number of the baskets corresponds to the number of these special community ministers. The baskets not only show the magnitude of the miracle: they also symbolically show that the apostles and disciples are to distribute to the community of believers the "bread" that is "left over" from Jesus' direct ministry (Schürmann 1969, 519)

The marvel of the deed is the effect of Jesus' blessing. There is a striking parallel between Mark 6:41–42 and the words of the institution of the Eucharist in Mark 14:22–23. In the account of the multiplication of the loaves we read: "Taking (*labōn*) the five loaves (*artous*) . . . Jesus raised his eyes to heaven, pronounced a blessing, broke the loaves, and gave them to the disciples (*eulogēsen kai kateklasen . . . kai edidou*). . . . He divided the two fish among all of them (*pasin*)." And in the institution of the Eucharist: "He took bread (*labōn arton*), blessed and broke it, and gave it to them (*eulogēsas eklasen kai edōken*) . . . and passed it to them and they all (*pantes*) drank. . . ."

The Greek words can only be explained by their Semitic substrate. "To take" is a literal translation of *lāqaḥ*. A table blessing began by the taking of bread into one's hands (Jeremias 1966, 174). *Eulogēsen*, "pronounced a blessing," corresponds to the Hebrew *bārak*. All blessings began, "Blessed be you, Yahweh our God, king of the universe," and no Jew could partake of a meal before this blessing had been pronounced (Beyer 1964–76, 2:754–63). "To distribute bread" was not idiomatic Greek in classical times. "Distribute" is a translation of the verb *bāsā*, which was the technical term for the Jewish practice of distributing bread before the beginning of a meal (Jeremias 1966, 176).

In this scene we are in the midst of a mental world that is Semitic. This is no ordinary banquet. The form in which this meal is described comes down to us only in the accounts of the institution of the Eucharist and in texts influenced by these accounts. There is no convincing evidence that our detailed description of the rite of grace before meals, with the three key verbs of our two accounts, has any analogy with contemporary texts detailing the Jewish rite (Schürmann 1969, 158).

Before pronouncing the benediction—or effectuating the multiplication of the loaves—Jesus lifts his eyes to heaven. Before he acts, he enters into communication and concert with his Father (Jn 11:41, 17:1). This miraculous deed of his is the fruit of his familiarity with his Father. Standing before the helpless, Jesus has the same love for them as has his Father. Christian tradition relates the multiplication of the loaves in the same terms as the institution of the Eucharist because it sees such a wonderful parallel between the two events. Both are meals taken by Jesus with the community. Both are acts of service and dedication to the poor (Acts 2:42-47). And both are anticipations of the definitive, eschatological feast (Mk 14:25) in which all the poor and despised will partake of the very gladness of God.

Jesus closes this wondrous day by retiring to the mountain alone to pray (Mk 6:46). All Jesus' key decisions and deeds are accompanied by prayer. He prefers to pray in solitude (Mk 1:32, 14:32-39), in places far from the centers of power and oppression, where nothing can disturb his concentration on his conversation with his Father.

JESUS IN LEAGUE WITH SATAN?

A Strange Person

Jesus does not do as others do. Above all, he does not do as the leaders do. His teaching is not like that of those schooled in the Law (Mk 1:22). Neither is his life like theirs. He does not scruple to touch a woman ill with a fever (1:31) or a leper, who was considered to be the object of God's curse (1:40-45). He proclaims divine pardon without stint or limit (Mk 2:1-10; Lk 15:1-32). He speaks of God and refuses to live the rigorism of the pietists (Mk 2:18). He is on familiar terms with those enjoying the least prestige, and he joins in their celebrations (Mk 2:15-16). He even admits one of these corrupt persons to the circle of his intimate friends (2:14). Indeed he places the material needs of sick and helpless human beings above all laws and institutions (2:23, 3:6). Jesus "climbs out of his box." He inflames people's hopes for a way of life to which they are not accustomed, and in so doing he suspends everybody's pet securities.

Neither tradition nor personal and family interests suffice to explain his behavior. Generally people were not pleased by his conduct, not even his family (Jn 7:5). He must be mad—at least this is the only explanation his family can imagine (Mk 3:21), and they try to prevent him from further public appearances.

A Strange Community

The first Christians, too, disturbed prevailing mores. For them too the kingdom of God, the triumph of God's justice and love here on earth and forever after, was more important than tradition (Mt 5:21-48), family (Mk 1:16-20), or property (Mk 10:22-30). It was more important than any kind of security or comfort (Mk 8:34-37); indeed it was more important than health and life itself.

This manner of life upset all prevailing values. The greatest person is the one who serves (Mk 9:35, 10:43-44), and the one whose favor had better be courted is the person who is as helpless and dependent as a child (9:37). When you come right down to it, the first Christians' life ideal was to live the impossible (10:27).

Many, even near relatives, might well regard this as madness. Acceptance of such a lifestyle entailed painful separation and rejection, rejection even by one's own family (13:12-13). But in running the risk of this rejection, the first Christians were only following in the footsteps of Jesus. Their hard life did not lead to pure suffering, nor was it intended to. They were not seeking pain for pain's sake. It is only that this is the lifestyle that makes us members of Jesus' family (3:31-35). In Jesus we come to know the will of God—God our friend, God the ally of the outcast (1:40–45), the rejected (2:15–17), the hungry (2:23–28), the helpless (3:1–6). By accepting a liberating God and by placing that God above all other interests and relationships (Lk 14:26–33) and above all one's security (Mk 8:34–37) and all one's inclinations (Mk 14:36), one becomes part of the mightiest community of brothers and sisters imaginable. Those who live in this way are Jesus' true family, in which everyone has value, all are equal (Mk 9:36–40, 10:30; Mt 23:8–12), and the categories of dehumanizing societies are turned topsy-turvy (Mk 10:30, 42–44). Those who do not accept this way of life are outside Jesus' circle—strangers to Christ—because for him what ultimately counts is God's will, which is all justice and all love (Mk 14:36; Mt 6:1–15).

Subverting the Prevailing Order

All those who strive to follow Jesus will be insulted, accused, threatened, and branded as destroyers of civilization, as lovers of disorder and violence, and of course as enemies of God. Actually, they are only attempting to put an end to all forms of oppression and violence—to do away with the idolatry of power and money, the deification of ambition and caprice, and the subjection of the weak to force and selfishness. Such persons condemn themselves to make use of every means in the struggle for all to live as daughters and sons of God, and these persons are bound not to depend on anything that runs contrary to the divine goodness.

This is the same as Jesus' own struggle, and accusations—as also in Jesus' case—are but a means of facilitating the extermination of those who seek with all their might to hasten the reign of God's justice and mercy. Of course, Jesus himself was exterminated. Hostility toward his manner of life is not purely intellectual. It may even be that reason is what counts least. This hostility is a value judgment, a decision in which one's whole existence is at stake. Before finally coming to reasons and facts, every other means is had recourse to, from calumny to ridicule. When the hostility is radical, it annihilates those who live as Jesus did.

Mark is telling Christians that they are not off course—that their difficulties are the same ones Jesus had. Christians suffer in this manner because they are following Jesus, and they ought to react as

Jesus reacted. Like the first Christians, Jesus was accused of being an instrument of Satan. His success, it was said, was the work of diabolical forces (Mk 3:22; Jn 10:20, 8:48) (Justin Martyr, *Dialogue with Trypho* 69. Cf. *Babylonian Talmud,* Sanhedrin 43a).

Confronted with this accusation, Jesus is not primarily concerned to defend himself. He does not deny the accusation explicitly. He uses figurative language. The form of his denial is more important than its content (Gnilka 1978, 1:149). His reply gets at what lies behind the accusation—he attacks the presuppositions that prevent the doctors of the law from accepting him (Tannehill 1975, 179). Jesus makes no attempt to be devastating, nor do nice theories interest him. His interest is in changing people. He wants to drive a wedge into this solid mass of prejudice. He wants his accusers to be able to ask themselves: But how is it possible for Satan to drive out Satan? (Mk 3:23). He wants them at least to be capable of discerning that their "reasons" are a cloak for their prejudices.

Jesus begins by taking their standpoint. He grants for the sake of argument that the accusation they are making is true. Then, based on simple data admitted by everyone, he carries their accusation to its ultimate consequences. He uses images, and uses them with stubbornness and repetition: "How can Satan expel Satan? If a kingdom is torn by civil strife, that kingdom cannot last" (Mk 3:23–24). Its division will be the prelude to total collapse (Dt 2:41, 11:4). Internal division will lead to collapse even in the smallest of organizations, the family (Mk 3:25).

Three times in Jesus' conditional discourse we hear the verb "cannot." Most emphatically, internal division brings about impotence and ruin. None of Jesus' hearers, not even the most ignorant among them, would have denied this fact.

In the third figure (Mk 3:26), we find significant grammatical changes, indicating that supposition has yielded to fact. The perfect symmetry of the first two figures is broken with an extra verb in the conditional mood, as well as an extra verb in the conclusion, the main clause. *Ean,* "if," the hypothetical conditional, becomes *ei,* the factual conditional. "If" Satan has *actually* risen up against himself and divided himself, he cannot stay on his feet, he is lost. In other words, either the accusation lodged against Jesus by his adversaries is a pure lie, and hence is morally disqualified, or it is legitimate, and then it must be admitted that what has happened with the coming of Jesus is wondrous indeed: the collapse of the kingdom of Satan, the ruin of whatever crushes and lessens a human being. In the presence of actions like those of Jesus, God can reign in all things and over all persons. Thanks to the deeds of Jesus, the divine will can be completely realized. But if Jesus' power is not a manifestation of evil, a sign of hatred of God, then where does his strength come from?

Mark welds together various phrases that correspond to the accusation brought against Jesus. At the center of the accusation we find verse 27. This little parable can be understood in isolation, but its place in the context connects it with the conclusion of Mark 3:26, and it makes that conclusion understandable as a proclamation of what Jesus is (Tannehill 1975, 182). Jesus is someone stronger than Satan, and he claims this Satan-conquering power as his own. Jesus' power, his strength, is the Holy Spirit. Jesus' deeds are deeds that deliver persons from dehumanizing power. They are manifestations of the lordship of God, and God wishes all human beings free and fulfilled.

Rejection and Repression

Jesus' followers, tortured and sentenced by the courts (Mk 13:9–11), were treated as scum (Lk 6:22) by a society that considered its cruel fury a homage to God (Jn 16:1–4). The lot of Jesus' followers was that of the prophets (Jer 12:6) and of Jesus himself (Jn 15:17–22). The prophets were no more believed than was Jesus (Mk 6:1–6).

The first Christians, who were subjected to so much hatred and rejection for Jesus' sake, reflected on what all this might mean (Jn 15:23–25). They based their reflection on the words of Jesus (Mk 3:28–29). Jesus showed and proclaimed God's love for all men and women (Mk 3:28; Lk 7:36–50, 15:1–32; Jn 8:2–11). Jesus preached God in word and in deed, and God rejects no one. God, who is joyful and respects all persons, seeks to be near everyone. For Jesus' God there are no enemies, no outcasts, no second-class citizens. Jesus' God, the God of grace, forgiveness, and life, is absolute availability to all human beings. Because they proclaim this unlimited, unconditional grace of God, Jesus and those who belong to him are rejected as enemies of God and society.

The deliberate blindness (Jn 9:41), the frenzy that is stirred up against the divine goodness (Jn 15:23-25), and the fanatical dedication to the destruction of the fallen and lowly (Mk 3:6) are elicited by God's beneficent workings through Jesus (Mk 3:6) and are the "satanization of God"—God who freely offers joy, freedom, and justice to all without exception. They are a direct insult to the Spirit of God. They are the clearly rationalized rejection of God's friendship and pardon. And that is why they are unpardonable.

This terrible warning (Mk 3:29) is a work of grace. It places us on our guard; it warns us before it is too late. "It's the devil doing it"—an old ploy if ever there was one, a coarse piece of stupidity we still hear in our own times. Let us remember, should we ourselves ever be tempted to support a like myth, that Jesus never preaches about Satan. He always preaches victory over Satan. Satan's power is a power over human beings that alienates and blinds them (Mt 6:13; Acts 26:18; Col 1:13) (Foerster 1964-76, 2:72-81). It dominates (Jn 12:31), deceives, and destroys people (Jn 8:44; Rev 12:10). It seeks to put men and women to death (Lk 13:11-16). It reduces them to slavery, leads them down to death (Acts 2:14). The power of Satan is whatever seeks to uproot what God has sown in human beings (Mk 4:15).

The experience of evil as a crushing reality is something we have all suffered. But the Christian faith is not exhausted by the experience. Rather it gives us the strength and courage to see the superhuman magnitude of evil, and accordingly to take it very seriously. Faith likewise gives us the strength to struggle against evil, lest we ever resign ourselves to its efforts to kill, diminish, and destroy persons. After all, there is "someone stronger" (Lk 11:22) than this seemingly invincible evil: Jesus of Nazareth, itinerant preacher, poor carpenter, and historical manifestation of the goodness of God toward all human beings (González-Faus 1977, 495-514).

Chapter 3

Jesus and the Oppressed

JESUS AND WOMAN

Women in the Time of Jesus

Women in Jesus' times were much more oppressed than they are today. To add insult to injury, the oppression was rationalized as compliance with the divine will. In Israel the husband was the wife's lord and master. Just as a girl was under the dominion of her father, so a married woman was under the dominion of her husband. The Ten Commandments as given in Exodus 20 treat wives as property: "You shall not covet your neighbor's wife, nor his male or female slave, nor his ox or ass, nor anything else that belongs to him" (Ex 20:17) (de Vaux 1961, 1:48). A wife even addressed her husband as *Adon* (Gn 18:12; Am 4:1)—the same title a slave used with a master or a subject with a king.

A father had the power to sell his daughter (Ex 21:7). Girls were frequently betrothed at twelve and a half years of age because this was the time when a father ceased to have total legal disposition of his daughter (Leipoldt and Grundmann 1973, 1:192). A father could even marry his daughter to a person who was deformed (*Babylonian Talmud,* Kethuboth 40b). In 1 Samuel 18 we have a clear instance of the exercise of the father's power. Saul had offered David the hand of his eldest daughter, Merob, on condition he show himself valiant in the battles he was to wage for the Lord. When the moment of the betrothal arrived, Merob was given to

Adriel the Meholathite instead. Michal, another of Saul's daughters, was in love with David, and she communicated this to her father. Saul congratulated himself, thinking that he could offer her to David as bait and that David would fall into the hands of the Philistines. So Saul betrothed his daughter Michal to David in exchange for a hundred Philistine foreskins.

We often read the phrase "women, [pagan] slaves, and minors" to indicate those who enjoyed incomplete rights (*Sukkah* 2:8 and *Berakhot* 3:3). Acquiring a wife was much like acquiring a slave. "A wife is acquired by money, documents, and coitus. . . . A pagan slave is acquired by money, documents, and retention" (*Qiddushin* 1:13). Indeed sometimes any difference in the form of acquisition was denied (Jeremias 1977, 379 n. 78).

Inasmuch as their legal status was that of private property, women were secluded. Women took no part whatever in public life. Unmarried women lived mostly shut up in their houses (2 Mc 3:19). In 4 Maccabees (18:7) the mother of the seven sons says: "I was virgin pure, and had never left my father's house."

Given the place and value ascribed to women in Hebrew society, we need not be surprised that Sirach 42:9 ff. considers a daughter a "treacherous treasure" and recommends that

> where she lives let be there no grate, nor any porches round about the entranceway; nor let her show her beauty to any man, nor engage in formalities with woman. For as the moth passes from garment to garment, so does evil from woman to woman.

Schools were for boys only. A woman's education was restricted to her apprenticeship in household tasks (Jeremias 1977, 374, 384). When a married woman left her house, she had to cover herself enough to prevent recognition. Otherwise she offended against accepted convention to the point that her husband had the right, and even the duty, to dismiss her without any obligation of paying her the sum stipulated in the marriage contract in case of divorce (Jeremias 1977, 372). Among the poor, rigorous seclusion was impossible. In Sadducean circles, as indeed among the leisure classes, the mentality was somewhat liberal (Leipoldt and Grundmann 1973, 1:192).

The women's atrium in the temple was fifteen steps below the man's atrium, and women were forbidden to ascend to the upper atrium (Leipoldt and Grundmann 1973, 1:190). A woman's word could not be admitted as evidence in court. A woman could inherit a legacy only in the absence of a male heir (Nm 27:8). The validity of a woman's contractual promise depended upon the will of the man to whom she was subject—her father or her husband (Nm 30:14–17). Anything a woman found by accident or produced by her own toil was the property of the male to whom she was subject. Women had to perform tasks (for the benefit of their husbands or fathers) that males performed only if they were gentile slaves (Leipoldt and Grundmann 1973, 1:194).

Sterility, which was attributed only to women, was looked upon as a divine punishment (Lk 1:25). The esteem in which a woman was held was in proportion to the number of her male children (see Gn 28:31–35) (de Vaux 1967, 1:68). A woman was totally subject to her spouse. "If she walks not by your side, cut her away from you" (Sir 25:25). Proverbs (5:15–19) recommends conjugal fidelity on the part of a husband, but his infidelity was not actually punished unless he offended against the right of another man by having sexual relations with a married woman (de Vaux 1967, 1:63). If a woman failed to maintain conjugal fidelity she was punished terribly: she would be either stoned to death or strangled. An adulterous woman was considered a "triple sinner," and her infamy could never be blotted out (see Sir 23:22–26). For Philo the greatest of crimes was adultery. It was the crime most odious to human beings and most repulsive to God (Hauck 1964–76b, 4:729–35). But of an adulterous couple, the woman was to be the more severely punished because adultery was a transgression against a man, not a woman. Polygamy was practiced, particularly by the rich.

No one in Israel questioned the licitness of divorce. If a man had got himself a wife then surely he could be rid of her. There were few legal restrictions on a husband's right in this regard. It was only the man who could divorce; the wife could only respect his decision. A woman could not sue for divorce. Deuteronomy (24:1) tells us that sufficient grounds for divorce could be the husband's merely having discovered "something indecent" in his wife. The expression came in for a great deal of rabbinical discussion, and for one rabbi (toward the end of the first century) the fact that a husband found another woman more beautiful obviously constituted something relatively indecent in his wife (Sifre Dt 269, or 24:1).

The Israelites considered divorce to be one of the privileges of Israel: "Only in Israel has God joined his name to divorce" (*Tosefta Qiddushin* 1:58c, 16 ff.). Here, then, was a form of oppression that had the endorsement of God. Some commentators have seen a defense of monogamy in Malachi 2:14–16. This passage, however, refers rather to the repudiation of a present wife: it does not actually deal with infidelity. A man was free to have a number of wives (Elliger 1956). Philo alone denies that it is obligatory to divorce a woman after ten years if she has not borne children because, as he says, the love pact still has validity (Oepke 1964–76, 1:776–89).

It was not only for divorce that religious justification was sought. Divine right was claimed for all forms of oppression against women. Women as such were considered inferior to men. Women, it would seem, were full of defects: they were deceitful; they were gossips; they were indolent and light-minded; and they practiced witchcraft. Accordingly, they deserved only contempt. Women were thought to be nymphomaniacal seductresses. It was commonly held that women were incapable of observing the commandments, inasmuch as they were considered to lack the capacity for schooling (*Babylonian Talmud,* Shabbat 33b). They were not taught the scriptures. Indeed Rabbi Eliezer, toward the end of the first century, stated: "Anyone schooling his daughter in the Torah is schooling her in its abuse" (Jeremias 1977, 384, n. 128, citing Sota 3). Small wonder, then, that Rabbi Judah ben Ilay prayed: "Praise be [O Lord], that thou didst not make me a woman!" (Leipoldt and Grundmann 1973, 191, citing *Tosefta Berakot* 7:18).

Among the gentiles, too, contempt for women was cultural and ingrained. In the first place, in a world of slavery there were people with whom you could do anything you wished. In the second place, prejudices against women were very strong, and the privileges accorded a male by reason of his sex were considerable. For Sophocles, woman was only the highest of the beasts (Sophocles, *Fragment* 488 [1963], 1:44). Speaking of the role of woman in society, Pseudo-Demosthenes wrote: "We have *hetairai* for solace, concubines for our bodily needs, and wives for legitimate sons" (Pseudo-Demosthenes, *Orationes* 59, 122).

Divorce was frequent in Greece: "As a rule, men married eleven or twelve women, one after the other. One who had only married four or five times was accounted a veritable catastrophe, a pitiable bachelor (Menander, *Fragments* 794–95 [547–48] [1959], 2:247): For the Romans the procedure in case of adultery was crystal clear. If a man found his wife in adultery, he could simply kill her, without judicial process and with impunity. If it was the male who had committed adultery, his wife did "not dare lay a finger on [him]" (Hauck 1964–76b).

Only women were expected to practice marital fidelity unconditionally. Even the most strictly religious marriage—the *confarreatio*—could be dissolved "if the wife does anything evil or repugnant," which in practice meant "if the husband feels like marrying someone else."

Just as Roman women took a comparatively active part in civil life, so too they could sue for divorce, and they very frequently did. In fact, mores being generally relaxed, Roman women were generally very free with their marital infidelities (Martial LV, 71, cf. Seneca, *De Beneficiis* 3, 16, 2, 3 [1961], 1:74–75).

Christians and Women

Sooner or later, Christians were going to have to ask themselves what attitude they were to take in this atmosphere so stifling and destructive for women. They would want to know whether their faith in Jesus implied accommodation or breach with this world of opprobrium and degradation for half of the human race. And of course they would seek their answer in Jesus' words.

God's Will or Hardheartedness?

In the Palestine of the time of Jesus, one would think it would have been impossible to doubt the legitimacy of divorce—that clear expression of man's dominion over women. And yet this is the very question put to Jesus by the Pharisees (Mk 10:2). The evangelist adds that their purpose was to put him to the test. If Jesus denied the legitimacy of divorce, he would be placing himself in contradiction with the Law of Moses. In other words, he would be subverting the social and religious order of his people.

This line of questioning would have been as strange to the

Hellenistic world as it must have been to the Judaic. I fail to see how the incisive formulation of our text could have been the fruit of any reflection on the part of the primitive Christian community that did not ultimately go back to Jesus. No, this question must have been put to Jesus because of something that Jesus had said. We note that the question is posed by those who have already judged their adversary guilty of blasphemy, diabolical possession, violation of the traditions, and behavior generally deviating from established norms. They have already decided to have Jesus put to death. Evidently they see the possibility, in the response they hope to have from their new question, for one more reason to have him put to death. He is a total challenge to their way of thinking and living.

The Pharisees base the licitness of divorce on Moses' concession to the people recorded in Deuteronomy 24:1. This verse provoked an incredible tangle of controversy and discussion as to its exact meaning, but the validity of divorce was never questioned. It was seen as the law of God. For Jesus, this concession was not an expression of the will of God; it only demonstrated human beings' hardness of heart. Hardness of heart was stubbornness indeed, but it was more than an emotional deficiency; it was a vital attitude, a very particular manner of reacting to God.

Hardness of heart is diffidence with respect to God, a refusal of dedication to God, the just judge, the protector of the poor (Dt 10:16–18). Hardness of heart means taking no account of the Lord (Ez 3:7), unwillingness to commit oneself to truth, justice, and the Lord's rights (Jer 4:2–3). The disposition of Deuteronomy 24:1 is evidence against (in Greek, *pros*) the Jews' hardness of heart: obviously they were incapable of persevering in a permanent marriage (Schnackenburg 1971, 418).

Jesus deprives Deuteronomy's disposition on divorce of all its force by appealing not to God but to the stubbornness, the resistance, of those who oppose God: those who are Jesus' very hearers. He thereby falls under their condemnation. He has "despised the word of God," as the *Babylonian Talmud* (Sanhedrin 99a) puts it, and hence would "not share in eternal life."

For Jesus, a man has no right to dominate a woman. Nothing justifies "having" a woman as an object, a possession. In practice a well-stocked harem and divorce were privileges of the wealthy. Even when a poor man took a second wife it was for economic reasons—to gain a servant or to get sons (de Vaux 1967, 1:46–47, 62). For Jesus, the divorce law is destined to perish. For Jesus, this disposition of Moses is in violation of God's original plan. For Jesus, the moment has arrived to do away with narrow categories and begin to live the perfect order of times in total fidelity to God's demands.

Jesus reminds his audience of the order of creation and the elementary, inviolable unity of that creation (Stauffer 1964–76, 1:648–57). It is God who made the human being male-and-female (Gn 1:17). In other words, the male being and the female being, masculine sexuality and feminine sexuality, are made by God so that neither can be understood without the other. Jesus places the female human being and the male human being on the same level, which for him is the only level God intends.

Claus Westermann is absolutely correct in holding that any privilege whatever, be it theoretical or intellectual, of the male human being over the female, any line of demarcation between male and female, endangers the doctrine of creation proclaimed in Genesis 1:27 (Westermann 1976, 221).

Jesus underscores the effect of this God-given bisexuality. Its effect is the union of man and woman. The male was created for the female and the female for the male. Neither economic or social motives nor the need to propagate the species must prevail in this union. They are not its explanation. Love, mutual attraction, is its prevailing element and explanation. The irresistible force of this life is anchored in the will of God, who created the sexes in complementarity and made them necessary for each other. God has intended them as a single reality, destined them to live in personal commitment and reciprocal dedication (Mk 10:8–9). God's plan is to unite man and woman in love, and this is what is decisive for them.

If we put asunder the union of man and woman, we sunder ourselves from God's will (Mk 10:10). Jesus, by his reply, shows the Pharisees that they are incapable of understanding that will.

Beyond Moses: The Original Equality

In his message as in his person, Jesus ushers in a new era, one in which the marriage ideal will be a much more profound one. With Jesus, it is easily possible to live the creative will of God. With Jesus' praxis, all justification of the intent to subjugate a person by reason of sex has vanished. There is no longer any imaginable reason for considering a woman a possession or an object of amusement.

Jesus refused to reduce woman to her reproductive organ, to limit the union of husband and wife to carnal copulation. Jesus bases their union on identification, on community of lives, on personal dedication. Subjugation yields to equality. Possession fades away before the all-conquering reality of love. For Jesus, the love of man and woman is not a mere means but a relative end in itself. His vision springs from his experience of the reign of God. With Jesus a stage in human development—or nondevelopment—characterized by oppression of and contempt for woman is transcended.

The key phrase for this whole discussion is in verse 9 of the tenth chapter of Mark: "Therefore let no man separate what God has joined" (Tannehill 1975, 97). To repudiate one's wife is to repudiate God's will.

Our scene could have been finished, complete, and fully intelligible with this verse. But Mark goes on to have Jesus link divorce and adultery. Matthew 5:32, 19:9, and Luke 16:18 report the same logion almost word for word. Of course, a slight difference in wording implies a slight difference in meaning. In Mark's Gospel it is the husband who is committing adultery against his wife. Matthew (5:32) has the man who repudiates his wife forcing his wife to commit adultery. Matthew sees the problem altogether from a masculine point of view, which is probably closer to what a Palestinian Jesus, or his spokesperson, actually said (Vawter 1977, 532). But no such difference in emphasis undermines the intimate bond Jesus posits between divorce and adultery. Divorce was actually required by law. Adultery was severely punished. The upshot of this paradoxical situation was that the husband was easily exonerated of his responsibility, and the burden of the sin fell to the wife. Putting husband and wife on the same plane was absurd for the male-chauvinist mentality of the time.

A Call for Women's Rights

That adultery should be an offense against a woman was unthinkable in both the Jewish and the Greco-Roman worlds. Jesus is not just giving people an extra law to obey. He is shaking the conscience of a "macho" society to its very foundations. Mark

10:12 is simply inconceivable in the context of Jewish society of the time: "And the woman who divorces her husband and marries another commits adultery." The reason, of course, is very simple: in Judaism divorce was the exclusive privilege of the husband.

A short phrase provides us with a key to understanding the statement attributed to Jesus, a statement so at odds with the mentality of the times. I refer to the expression *eis tēn oikian,* "back at the house." Suddenly we find ourselves in circumstances similar to those of Mark 4:10–13, 7:17–18, and 9:28–29. The literary structure of the expression, hence very likely its theological function, is the same. The question put to Jesus and Jesus' reproach clearly indicate that the explanation we are about to hear is a commentary on the verses that have gone before (Minette de Tillesse 1968, 229). In all four passages we have a scene that is complete, finished—and then all of a sudden the disciples ask the key question all over again (230). In the passage concerning divorce, for example, the decisive answer has been received and the case seems closed with Mark 10:9. Then, inexplicably, it is reopened. Besides that there is a change of tone in verses 10:12. Jesus' tone is no longer scriptural or messianic. It is pastoral (Minette de Tillesse 1968, 231). The same change of tone is observable in the other three Markan passages just mentioned.

Jesus is in Judea or Transjordan (Mk 10:1) up until verse 10. Then suddenly he is "back at the house"! Lest we be forced to hypothesize that the house was following them around, let us try to grasp the theological procedure here and not merely follow a minutely detailed travelogue.

Again and again in Mark's Gospel Jesus is seen speaking with his disciples in private. Scholarship finds a "redactional intervention," an editor's comment, here (Minette de Tillesse 1968, 239). "The house" in Mark has a theological meaning. It is the place where Jesus meets his disciples intimately and can therefore manifest his messianic confidences more explicitly, far from the crowd (245). The disciples "back in the house" are Jesus' new family (248). Jesus' disciples are the only persons who are able to understand the whole scope of his doctrine and person (cf. Mk 9:9–13, 13:3).

In Mark 10:10–12, then, we have a new, unexpected demand put upon those who wish to live as disciples of Christ. They must be able to see what "outsiders" cannot: that in the community founded by Jesus a carnal love can be lived that is free of any fraud or deceit, free of any lust for domination. In the church, Jesus' followers see the place where love can live uncrippled, where a man and a woman can express a love so powerful and so pure that they come to be a single reality.

If Mark 10:12 is an adaptation of the words of Jesus to the Roman world, which seems very likely, the passage is also showing us how the first Christians perceived the presence of Jesus in the church. For them Jesus was not a memory. Jesus was speaking to them in the practice of the faith and in the hope of the church. Jesus' abrogation of divorce is unquestionably complete and total, but he does not impose it as a law. This type of conjugal union —one husband with one wife forever—can only be a result of the acceptance of the reign of God, the fruit of faith in the gospel.

WHAT IS A POOR PERSON WORTH?

What Is of Real Value: God in the Hearts of the Poor

Within and without Judaism, people have always wondered about the real value of a religious offering. There has always been the danger of seeking to purchase the divine benevolence, of making money the driving force of religion. To this everlasting temptation, clear-sighted morality and religion have always replied: "How often I have seen the poor being more sensible than the rich, offering with their own hands little gifts to the gods, but with more devotion than those who cause bullocks to be led to sacrifice!" (see Lee 1971, 344).

Judaism not only prescribed that an offering be in accordance with each person's economic capacity and that it be made with a right intention, but also maintained that God considers the offering of a poor person as equivalent to the offering of that person's very life (Strack and Billerbeck 1922–28, 2:45). We need only recall the famous passage of *Leviticus Rabba* (3, 107a):

On a certain day, a woman brought an offering of a handful of flour. But the priest condemned it, saying: "See what this one has brought us! How much eating will that make? What kind of offering is that?'' But then the priest heard this in a dream: ''Despise it not, for it is as if that person had offered her life.''

At first glance, it might appear as if Jesus were doing nothing more than repeating this wise piece of religious discernment. Indeed it would be quite a plus if Christians would accept even this, with all its practical consequences.

Within the brief account of the widow's mite—barely four verses—a number of words with an economic connotation attract our attention: *gazophulakion,* with its double meaning of ''trea-sury'' and ''collection box'' (Mk 12:41 [twice], 43), ''money'' (v 41), ''few cents'' (v 42), ''sizable amounts'' (v 41), ''putting money,'' or ''contributed,'' ''donated,'' ''gave'' (vv 41 [twice], 42, 43, 44 [twice]), ''poor widow'' (vv 42, 43), ''more than'' (v 43), ''surplus wealth,'' ''want,'' what ''she had to live on'' (v 44). It sounds like a ledger but it is nothing of the kind. The rich are numerous, and they give a great deal of their money. By contrast a widow, needy and alone, drops a paltry sum in the box. Great emphasis is placed on the widow's situation in life: she has nothing—no one or anything she can count on. The abundance of the rich appears side by side with the want, the misery, of the widow. This person's situation is worse than that of the scribes' victims (Mk 12:40), for she no longer has anything they can take from her.

In the temple, where Israel's authorities and guides deal in business with, make a business of, religion (Mk 11:17), this forlorn widow makes a greater contribution than all the wealthy together. She gives something the rich cannot give. Jesus' interpretation of the widow's conduct subverts the whole notion of religious book-keeping.

In contrast with the lawyers' lifestyle (Mk 12:38–40), Jesus points to the destitute widow as a model. It is from her that the disciples are to learn something. Among those like her God's true people are to be found. These are the people who love God with their whole being (Mk 12:4, 12:28–30). The widow knows how to offer true worship to God (12:33). She is a full-fledged citizen of the kingdom of God (12:34).

In contrast with the sterility of official religion, which gets along on miracles and money alone (Mk 11:12–22), the poor widow demonstrates true faith in God (11:22–24). Her strength and her security are God (12:44). The interpretation Jesus and the first Christians make of this poor person's behavior is an absolute and utter reversal of values, a contradiction of everything that motivates a class society, a commercial society. For this poor person, as for the poor Jesus and the poor primitive communities, what counts is God.

"I Want You to Observe": The Gulf Is Unbridgeable

What the widow deposited in one of the temple collection boxes was an absolutely paltry sum. The coins she placed in the box were the smallest in circulation. What she gave was useless from an economic standpoint: it could never have improved the temple finances (Simon 1969, 123). The rich give a great deal, and with a flourish. Faced with the striking contrast, Jesus decides to delve into it with his disciples, so that they may see what he thinks about the matter and come to grasp the importance it has for them who hope to have a share in the kingdom of God (Mk 6:7, 7:14, 8:1, 34, 10:42). And so he calls them to gather around him and listen.

What Jesus says is a revelation to the disciples. "I want you to observe," he begins—*Amēn legō humin,* "Amen, I say to you" —using the stock introductory formula for the communication of a teaching about the relationship of behavior with the kingdom of God. The same expression occurs in Mark 3:28, 9:41, and 14:9. This formula always serves notice that we are about to hear what One to whom the final outcome, the definitive answer, has been revealed—the ultimate meaning of events—understands as to the real importance of some action (Berger 1970, 480).

For Jesus, what the rich give is religious compromise. They give nothing—less than two cents. The rich lose nothing, risk nothing. They give God from their superfluity. What the widow gives is what she has to live on. She gives herself to God altogether. God is the basis and foundation of her whole life. It is God on whom she counts for facing the uncertainties of her future. She has placed her whole existence in the hands of God. The difference between the widow and the rich is not one of degree but of kind. The gap is measureless.

The widow does what any follower of Jesus must do: have absolute confidence in God (Mk 11:22–24). What God is for the widow, God must also be for the follower of Jesus; incomparably more than power, more than money, more than everything (Mk 11:15; 12:40). If you follow money, you cannot follow Jesus (10:22). You cannot get into the kingdom of God with money (10:25).

Chapter 4

Confrontation with the Powers

JESUS AND WEALTH

Skirting the Issue: The Interpreters

There has always been tension in Christian communities where money is concerned. We do not all share the same attitude toward money, nor indeed is there conformity between what we believe and what we do. We read the idyllic description of a community that possessed everything in common, in which no one wanted for anything and joy reigned supreme (Acts 2:42–47, 5:1–11, 6:1–7). But we also read the coarse truth about a division caused by economic distinctions among the members of a Christian community (1 Cor 11:20–22; Jas 2:1–9).

It goes without saying that—living in a society where wealth was an object of adoration—the Christian community would have to make a clear statement of its position regarding the accumulation of wealth (Jas 5:1–6) and that it would seek to base its solution on something Jesus has said.

It would be less than honest to deny the passion with which this subject is treated. On the one side, we have those who refuse to let anything even remotely threaten their privileged positions. On the other, there are commentators who feel an almost unutterable loathing in the face of the inequities and misery that people have had to suffer because of the inevitable injustice of the wealthy.

And so the word *rich* in the Bible has been interpreted

figuratively. Thus the "rich" are not those who possess capital or control the means of production. No, the "rich" must be the haughty or people "attached" to money or those who "think they're somebody." An objective fact is translated into a subjective emotion, something individual and internal.

Next we get a "snarled" language. We hear about the "poor rich," and the "rich poor"—those who are rich in money but "poor in spirit," and those who, on the contrary, are poor in money but "rich in pride." We hear of those who have many things but who conduct themselves before God as if they did not—and we hear of those who "do not have a mat to die on" but who are filled with impediments to receiving the word of God. Suddenly words no longer serve a purpose—or better, their purpose is to confuse. The symptom that betrays the syndrome is that this metamorphosis is not applied to other words. It is not applied to "wise," for example, or "leader" or "virgin" or "friend."

The passage in Mark's Gospel that directly treats the subject of wealth (10:17–31) has been subjected to this hermeneutic violence. For example, instead of "camel" (*kamēlos*) we read in one manuscript "rope" (*kamilos*). The Beza and Koridethi codices, among others, use the phrase "those who put their trust in riches" instead of simply "the rich" as the original has it—thereby leading the reader to understand that there are some wealthy persons who will have no trouble inheriting eternal life. Many an old-time preacher explained that the "needle's eye" was one of the gates of Jerusalem (so named from its shape) and because it had not been erected to accommodate the passage of anything as tall as a camel, camels had to crouch a bit in order to squeeze through. The moral? If you are rich, you need a dose of humility. The difficulty with this interpretation, of course, is that not a shred of documentary evidence supports it.

According to Rudolf Bultmann, a scholar in the vanguard of Protestant exegesis, of all the material in Mark 10:23–26, the only historically authentic part is the disciples' question, "Then who can be saved?" (v 26). Middle-class Christians can sleep peacefully then. Of course Bultmann fails to explain how it would have been possible for that community of bumpkins, with their narrow perspective, to invent such powerful images (Bultmann 1961, 5ff.).

The Jesuit exegete A. Capelle believes that Jesus is speaking of the general difficulty of entering into the kingdom of God. His original message, we are told, is all in verse 24: "My sons, how hard it is to enter the kingdom of God!" Having to leave one's wealth and give it to the poor is of little importance. What Jesus is asking is something purely internal—a spiritual attitude. And here, we are told, is where Jesus' message reaches its zenith. Actually, it reaches it nadir, for now it has totally evaporated (Capelle 1975, 237). An interpretation like the preceding is a subterfuge.

It cannot have been an easy task to give our passage this interpretation. See how many things have to be forgotten. Verse 24 has to be totally divorced from its context. The verb *repeated,* which connects this verse with what has gone before, has to be ignored. And, finally, the touching expression of endearment, "my sons," has to be left out of account. With this last vocative, Jesus is laying special emphasis on something he is revealing, something close to his heart. We must keep in mind that verse 24b is practically a verbatim repetition of verse 23b—and that the next verse, 10:25, clearly states *who* will have enormous difficulties in entering the kingdom of God (Reploh 1969, 193).

Further, the disciples' question concerning who can be saved is not a generalized one. It is asked in the context of what has been said in the preceding verses, as the Greek particle, *de,* clearly shows: "They (*hoi de*) were completely overwhelmed at this, and exclaimed to one another, 'Then who can be saved' " (Mk 10:26). Our translation fails to reflect the force of this particle. The particle *de,* especially with the relative pronoun *hoi* ("they"—literally, "who"), serves to make a connection with what has just been stated. It means *autem,* "but," in the sense of the connective "now. . . ." The disciples' question, therefore, is to be understood in the context of the verses that have immediately preceded.

Are we surprised at the strangeness of Jesus' doctrine? We may take heart. The disciples themselves were astounded and dismayed. They "could only marvel" (10:24); "they were completely overwhelmed" (10:26). Jesus' clarity, insistence, and radicalism regarding wealth was a shock to them, too. Their emotion, their consternation, is extraordinary. It was the same emotion they felt when they saw Jesus walk on the water (Mk 6:51). Pilate will feel like this when he sees the people's frenzy and Jesus' silence (Pesch 1976, 2:143). Mark's verbs for all these reactions, all this stupefaction, ring like thunder. Here the disciples *ethambounto*, "marvel" (10:24) and *exeplēsonto*, "are overwhelmed" (10:26). When they saw Jesus walking on the water, they *etarachthēsan*, "were terrified" (Mk 6:50). Pilate's reaction was *thaumazein*, "surprise" (15:5). But our commentators somehow feel they must do away with anything that might astonish in Jesus' teaching.

Nor may we appeal to the subterfuge that the expression of the disciples' astonishment is a literary device. True, the disciples were not wealthy people. But it is also true that they were absolutely certain that without any money they could do nothing for people (Mk 6:37). Peter even "remonstrated" with Jesus for behaving in such a way as to leave the little group of companions with nothing, not even their lives (8:32). Love like that made Peter furious. Again, the disciples' great concern was who would be first among them. They had scant wish for a world of equals (9:33–34)! They sought to control everything, to have disposition of everything, just as if they had been wealthy (9:38). They put on airs; they scolded children (10:13). They sought to occupy the first places; they hoped to be able to act just as oppressors and tyrants do (10:35–45).

Scriptural Meaning of "Rich"

There is nothing in our passage (Mk 10:17–31) to suggest a spiritualistic meaning for the word *plousios*, "rich" or "wealthy." The wealthy young person who approaches Jesus *must sell what he has and give the proceeds away*. He has many possessions (10:21–22). A rich person is one who has capital (v 23). *Ktēma* (Acts 2:45, 5:1; Mt 19:22) was used to designate a piece of land, property, whether a field of grain, a pasture, or simply virgin land. In the plural, *ktēma* meant "lands" in the sense of a farm (Taylor 1966, 430). It must be kept in mind that agriculture was for all practical purposes the only means of production in the Palestine of Jesus' time, except in Jerusalem, and that it was therefore the basis of all capital. *Chrēmata* (Acts 4:37, 8:18, 20, 24:26) referred to wealth or capital (Rostovtzeff 1941, 2:1125–26).

Plousios never has any other meaning, in any of the gospels. The parable of Lazarus shows the rich person to be the one who can dress in luxury and give splendid banquets while the poor person is the one who has neither food nor clothing (Lk 16:19–21). The rich person controls the means of production, has many goods (which have been hoarded over the years), and can live the good life without working (Lk 12:13-21). Farm animals belonging to the wealthy are better fed than some people are and are better treated than farm laborers (Lk 15:16). Those who amass wealth for themselves can make "generous" offerings (Mk 12:41) and still maintain their lifestyle (Mk 12:44). They can bestow favors that will guarantee them special preference (Lk 14:12).

The meaning of the word *rich* is the same in the Old Testament. It means those who grow wealthy, who thrive, who grow sleek and prosper. These are fraudulent people: they ruin others; they fail to defend the cause of the poor (Jer 5:26-28). Ezekiel denounces Israel's great impurity: the leaders are destroying the people; the poor are victims of violence everywhere, to the end that their tormenters become even richer. The wealthy strike, crush, rob, and exploit those in need (Ez 22:24-29).

For Micah, the wealthy are filled with violence. For him too the rich are those who amass goods, by means of fraud and other acts of injustice (Mi 6:9-12). The rich person is the one who can live comfortably without having to work (Sir 11:16-19).

In the Ethiopian Book of Henoch we have a clear description of what a Jew understood by the "rich": those who have the capital, who possess everything they desire, who have hoarded up money and goods, and who have numerous laborers in their service (97:8-10). The First Book of Henoch tells us that rich people gobble up the best wheat, drink wine in abundance, can let their appetites run wild, trample the lowly under foot, and oppress the just (96:4, 5, 8).

We can see from these texts that for the people of the Old Testament, and for certain Palestinian religious groups wealth is not a matter of moral indifference. Wealth intrinsically involves exploitation and violence. This characteristic of wealth is denounced, in all its raw reality, by Amos (2:6, 7-12, 8:4-18) and other prophets of the same milieu.

Meaning of "Rich" in Hellenized Judaism

With the Hellenistic invasion the social and spiritual situation of the Jewish people changed. The invaders—military people, bureaucrats, merchants—were marked by the colonial mentality of the time. They were selfish. They were materialists. They had little idealism. Their morals were lax. All they wanted was a life of peaceful and easy pleasure and a minimum of concern and toil. Their main preoccupation was to multiply their possessions and bequeath them to their descendants. Marriage was a simple commercial transaction (Rostovtzeff 1941, 2:1125-26).

Foreign as such a view of life was to the whole tradition of Israel, with the conquest it began to extend to Palestinian cities and upper classes. The economy was modernized, but for the lower social strata and the rural population economic development only meant new exploitation and their situation actually deteriorated (Hengel 1973, 106). The upper classes and the empire joined forces and together oppressed the people. The situation is reflected in the Book of Jubilees (23:19 ff.): the poor, we are told, cried out against the rich on the basis of the Law and the Covenant. The lowly had to struggle against the great, and those who lived on "charity" had much to suffer at the hands of the mighty. The wealthy gradually adopted the customs of the empire. Indeed they gradually became paganized, and their interests came to be opposed to those of the Covenant of the Lord. Accordingly, it is scarcely to be wondered at if the typical Israelite opposition of the impious rich and the pious poor and oppressed lends itself to a spiritualistic interpretation (Hengel 1973, 114, 97ff). This interpretation will appear in certain late psalms (149), in the later parts of Proverbs (1:11-19, 3:31), and in the last prophetical texts (Zec 10:3-7, 11:4-17). In Qoheleth (the Book of Ecclesiastes) and at the time of the Maccabean rebellion especially, this interpretation enters an acute stage. But even within this spiritualizing interpretation, the rich person is still the one who exploits, who amasses goods, and who lives the good life.

In the later parts of the Old Testament, wealth is considered something good (Eccl 7:11). It brings ease and joy (Ecc 2:4-10), seals friendships (Prv 14:20, 19:24), brings peace (Sir 31:8), respect (Sir 10:30), and honor and glory (Sir 44:18). The causes of wealth are sobriety (Sir 19:1), perseverance (Prv 13:11), industry (Prv 10:4), experience (Prv 24:4), good sense (Prv 3:16-17, 8:18), humility, and reverence toward the Lord (Prv 10:4). The ultimate cause, however, of wealth is the divine blessing (Prv 10:22).

For late Judaism it is God who gives health and wealth. Before all else, God gives these as a reward for the fulfilling of the commandments (Hauck and Kasch 1964–76, 6:318–32). Wealth enables ones to give alms, and "almsgiving saves one from death and expiates every sin" (Tb 12:9). Thus the Talmud declares that there are riches that positively harm their possessors and others that benefit them.

Alms and works of charity are held in esteem because they gain treasure in heaven. They bring gladness even in this world, and then they endure in the world to come (*Pe'ah* 1:1). They are equal in weight to all the commandments of the Torah (*Tosefta Pe'ah* 1:19). Of course, one must limit one's charity (*Babylonian Talmud, Aralim* 8:4). In order to be able to give alms, one must have possessions! And so one must not give too much.

Here we have a type of piety, of religiousness, in which wealth is an inalienable good. Inequality, then, is justifiable. Indeed, at the extreme end of the spectrum we shall have the Sadducees, for whom wealth is the greatest of divine gifts.

A Rich Person? Impossible!

For Jesus, wealth is not only a serious difficulty, it is an insuperable one as far as entering the kingdom of God is concerned (Mk 10:23–25). "It is easier for a camel to pass through a needle's eye than for a rich man to enter the kingdom of God" (v 25). The camel was the largest known animal, and the eye of a needle the smallest known aperture. The commentators are not well advised to try to imagine that Jesus said something else instead of "camel," merely on grounds of the strangeness of the image. Jesus often uses such deliberately strong images in order to underscore what he sees as the most patent of contradictions. For Jesus, the notion of the saving power of money—more concretely, "for a rich man to enter the kingdom of God"—is as preposterous as looking at the "speck in your brother's eye when you miss the *plank* in your own" (Mt 7:3; cf Lk 6:41), or "strain[ing] out the gnat and swallow[ing] the *camel*" (Mt 23:24). "There is an incompatibility between the possession of wealth and the acquisition of life eternal (Dupont 1969, 3:159). Yes, you might say that.

If we attend to the biblical texts, rich people are the ones who de facto have power over other human beings, the ones who by virtue of their very possessions are able to acquire more money. They are the ones whom we would call in modern terms accumulators of capital.

The final redaction of the Gospel underscores this reality: Jesus states that it is impossible for a rich person to enter the kingdom of God. In the face of the stupefaction this causes in his disciples, he not only does not soften his statement, he strengthens it. Now the disciples feel even more disconcerted than before. Jesus' thinking runs so counter to the usual mentality that it inevitably disorients those who are guided by the calcified, the established. What Jesus is offering is anything but the wide, clear road that "leads to damnation" (cf. Mt 7:13)!

In no other passage in Mark's Gospel do we have Jesus so stubbornly insisting on something. Nor do we ever encounter such emphatic opposition on the part of his disciples. For the prophets, the evil that lies in the accumulation of wealth is in the injustice which is necessarily entailed. Jesus was poor. He had no economic security. He had no home (Lk 1:59; Mt 8:20) and was rejected by society as the poor are always rejected (Mk 6:1-6). If someone wishes to follow him, that person must stop accumulating wealth, which perishes (Mt 6:19), and sacrifice everything for the kingdom (Mt 13:44-46). And Jesus' disciples really did suffer hunger (Mk 2:23). It is not a matter of mere detachment from the world. Jesus himself characterizes his mission as good news for the poor, as the setting of the oppressed at liberty, and as the proclamation of God's liberation from all oppression and threat (Lk 4:16-21). Nearness to the poor defines nearness to Jesus (Mt 25:31-46). Jesus' life is a total commitment to the poor, yet he is without demagogy.

For Jesus, it does not suffice to abstain from doing injury to others in order to enter the kingdom of God. Nothing can buy entrance to the kingdom, least of all money. Jesus reveals to the rich their fundamental lack (Mk 10:21). They will cease to want for anything when they cease to be rich, when all that they possess has been placed at the service of the poor. The treasure that has value before God is acquired by total devotion to the poor. No other treasure has a future. If they do not place all their goods at the disposition of the poor, they do not love the Lord their God with their whole heart and their whole soul and their whole mind and their whole strength, because for Jesus it is impossible to love both God and money (Mt 6:24) (Pesch 1976, 1:141). For Jesus, those who live trying to love both God and money cannot be his disciples, even if they observe other ethic norms (Mk 10:20) and recognize a certain greatness in Jesus (10:17). Wealth is the standard means of domination over and exploitation of others (Ambrozic 1972, 171). Therefore it is diametrically opposed to God's sovereignty.

For Jesus, obedience to the commandments can in no wise be separated from service to the poor. One cannot follow both Jesus and wealth. If one follows Jesus, one must be in the unconditional service of the poor. Indeed one must unburden oneself of wealth. Wealth, we see from the account of the rich young person, is no obstacle to *hearing* Jesus' call. But it prevents one from *responding* to it (Dupont 1969, 3:159).

To recapitulate: Jesus does not counsel the wealthy to engage in works of charity. Much less, to be sure, does he endorse the obligation—so commonly proclaimed in his time—to devote no more than one-fifth of one's fortune to charity (Jeremias 1977, 146). In radicalizing the meaning of love for God, Jesus likewise radicalizes the need for freedom from money and the necessity of giving it to the victims of wealth, the poor. Jesus' justice surpasses that of the scribes and the Pharisees (Mt 5:20). Jesus has not come to justify what sorrows and excoriates the poor. He has come to offer the concrete possibility of entering into the kingdom of God. With Jesus God's kingship and holiness (cf. Mt 6:33) have arrived among us.

The story of the rich young person is the single case in all the gospels in which Jesus explicitly rejects a person who desires to follow him. For Mark, the radical nature of the evil of amassing riches lies in this, that they throttle people so that it becomes impossible for them to answer Jesus' invitation. The whole meaning of existence for disciples of Jesus is determined by their attitude toward money.

God or Money?

The rhetorical crescendo running through Mark 10:23–25 and the concise, graphic intensity of the image in verse 25, scarcely need any explanation. And yet, curiously, Jesus' dialogue with the disciples continues (vv 26-27). Jesus contrasts the treacherous power of money, which leads to death, with the power of God, which leads to enduring life.

Gentiles of various social strata were now joining the Christian community. Jesus' challenging words must have been a sore point for them. The balance must have been delicate. On the one hand, the tendency to condemn all the rich automatically had to be avoided. On the other hand, the prophets had indeed attacked a social class and not isolated individuals.

Jesus' thinking would have been distorted, then, by the concept that the poor have absolute certainty of salvation while each and every rich person is condemned out of hand. No, for Mark, the great evil of wealth consists in this, that it prevents one from following Jesus—that is, it prevents one from living as a disciple of Jesus. At the same time, the second, and decisive, part of Jesus' reply—"With God all things are possible" (Mk 10:27)—is a notion that is met frequently enough in scripture (Gn 18:14; Jb 42:2; Zec 8:6; Lk 1:37; Mk 14:36). In three of these passages—those from Genesis, Zechariah, and Luke—we are told that the future event described, which is viewed as inconceivable in terms of human possibilities, is to be the work of God's faithfulness. God's loyalty can grant us what we do not even dare imagine. The future belongs to God, who has become involved with human beings and has made a commitment to them. God alone can effect the miracle of a rich person's salvation. He alone can give what wealth cannot.

The Way of the Cross: Complete Renunciation

Mark sets the theme of the cross in a framework: the inability of the disciples to understand what Jesus is trying to say to them (Mk 8:27–10:52) (Ambrozic 1972, 171). Mark insists on this theme because some people in the community were unwilling to accept all the conclusions that followed from Jesus' discipleship.

In the background of the disciples' incomprehension, and its principal cause, is the matter of the Passion. Specifically: our scene immediately precedes the third prediction of the Passion. Jesus' road to Jerusalem is his way of the cross. This teaching and his conduct lead to the cross—to his having to endure the hatred and the opposition of the lords of this world. In a world where women are dominated by men (Mk 10:1–12), children despised by adults (10:13–16), and the poor ignored—at best—by the rich (10:17–27), Jesus conditions our approach to the God of love on the respect and service we show precisely these oppressed persons and groups. By opposing the values of an oppressive society in such a burdensome and challenging manner, Jesus becomes a subversive. Accordingly, to follow Jesus means to follow him in suffering (Pesch 1976, 2:146). For the community that follows Jesus, the inversion and subversion of values becomes a matter of obligation.

According to most modern commentators, verses 28–31 have been attached to verses 17–27 of Mark 10 because of the affinity of their subject matter. We are hearing the reading of Jesus' words made by the community of his disciples. In verse 28, Peter, in the name of all the disciples, is reported as claiming to have left all things. This does not seem to reflect the historical situation of the disciples before Jesus' resurrection. During Jesus' lifetime on earth, breaking with property and family were not all that rigorously imposed on the disciples (see, for example, Mk 1:29, 4:1, 36). Further, notwithstanding the personal, concrete terms of Peter's question, Jesus' reply is reported in general, theoretical terms. Jesus' reply differs considerably in the Matthean and Lukan accounts. Therefore it is most probable that what we have here in Mark is a reflection of the Christian community's situation during or on the eve of a persecution. For Jesus' sake, the community has renounced both family and property, and it is natural that they should wonder what they had gained by following Jesus in so radical a fashion. Surely we are hearing a question springing from exhaustion, disillusionment, and resignation (Pesch 1976, 2:208).

The gospel writer seeks to respond to this uneasiness by referring to a saying of Jesus. Everything in Jesus' reply is oriented to guaranteeing eternal life to those who have renounced all things for his sake and have decided to live as he did. In other words, Jesus assures those who have decided to live as he that they will have the true life, the life that really counts.

It may well be, of course, that Jesus actually did promise his disciples a personal relationship a hundred times more rich than the ones they had renounced (Taylor 1966, 434). Surely Jesus, who had suffered so many attacks and had had to live under so much surveillance, could have foreseen that there would be hardship and persecution in store for those who lived as he. He promised them an experience of community in which all would be genuine brothers and sisters, and no one would lord it over the others.

The gospel writer was aware of the precariousness of the church's situation, and of the insufficiency of the life of that church as the final answer to a human being's burning desire for unlimited life (Tannehill 1975, 151). Mark insists that the reward, even during the persecution, will be a hundred fold. Yet he has little wish to stir up any naive enthusiasm in his fellow believers. The life of the church is hard, and it is marked by persecution.

At the same time, he shows us that we receive family and property in a manner different from the way in which we enjoyed these things before. He tells us of a different type of family relationship and a different type of property. It is as if he were saying: what you have received is much more than you have given up, and yet you fail to recognize what you already have (Tannehill 1975, 151).

Mark wants to make us see what wealth there is in the communion of sisters and brothers that is unique to Jesus' discipleship. The type of life described for us in Acts 2:42–47 and 4:32–37 is a true reward and a reason in itself for rejoicing.

Verse 10:31 of Mark is not found in the Lukan and Matthean parallels. Luke and Matthew instead place these words at the end of Jesus' statement about the narrow door (Lk 13:30) and at the end of the parable of the laborers in the vineyard (Mt 20:16). These words were not uttered by Jesus on the occasion Mark cites. Mark uses them to point up the ultimate consequences of following Jesus and thus to encourage those who do follow him.

As the values Jesus proposes and lives are subversive so also is the situation he promises and seeks to bring about. With the triumph of the kingdom of God, ranks will be totally reversed: the high and mighty will not be able to enter into the kingdom of God while anyone who "remain[s] the last one of all and the servant of all" (Mk 9:35; cf. 10:43–44)—those who renounce whatever makes one wealthy in this type of society in order to follow Jesus, those who have followed him to the supreme humiliation—will be "first" in the kingdom of God. Only they have a future. Theirs is the hope of enjoying the definitive triumph of God.

JESUS AND POWER

"Give to Caesar what is Caesar's, but give to God what is God's" (Mk 12:17). This saying of Jesus has met with a wide variety of interpretations by different commentators in different ages. During the last one hundred years we have used it to support the separation of faith and politics, making faith something purely interior and individual, and maintaining that politics should be conducted according to a special morality of its own—if indeed *morality* is the word to use. This interpretation has been disseminated by groups both on the right and on the left, even within the church. The church is not to "meddle in politics," not to "rock the boat." Of course, when you stop to think about it, it would not do much good to have faith if faith had nothing to say about something as necessary for building society as politics is. To avoid falling into an "Oh I already knew that!" trap, then, we must analyze our text calmly and at some length.

Beginning with Mark 12:12–13, it is no longer a question of Jesus defending his conduct. The question being asked here is an "ethical" question, a question about behavior in general. It is put to Jesus as to one who is a recognized expert. However hypocritically, Jesus' adversaries acknowledge him as a teacher and defer to him as such (12:19–32) (Stock 1978b, 493). His teaching, not his credentials, are called into question—and not as pure speculation but as a basis for conduct and behavior (Stock 1978b, 495 n. 28).

All the emphasis in the passage is on what Jesus says. There is nothing to distract our attention from his trenchant words. We do not even have any indications of time and place.

The Interests at Stake

Certain Pharisees, along with certain Herodians (members of Herod's party), sent by the Sanhedrin, come to Jesus to pose a captious question. Their inquiry is not about taxation in general, but only about the levy based on the census and on property—an especially odious tax for Jewish nationalists, indicating that the Romans considered the Jews and their belongings part of their right of conquest.

Both those who posed the question and their principals had already made their decision. The Herodians, being in collaboration with the occupying power, accepted the tax without comment. The Pharisees, too, had made their peace with Roman domination, with the stipulation that they be allowed "freedom of worship" (anachronistic?—if the shoe fits, wear it) and the continuance of their privileged position among the Jewish people.

The groups hate each other, but they have struck a bargain, in order to combat Jesus. They are closer to each other than to Jesus. They can manage to tolerate each other, but they cannot tolerate this Jesus, whose continued presence disturbs the absolute tranquillity of their regime of domination.

They flatter Jesus in order to conceal their intent. By calling Jesus "sincere" they hope to be able to conceal their own duplicity. They know that Jesus is honest, and Jesus knows that they are hypocritical (Mk 12:14–15). They know Jesus is no Zealot (11:1–11), just as they know that he has no connection with the Romans. They are only interested in getting him killed (11:18, 12:12). They approach Jesus as if the power he has received from God were a power like their own (8:11). They know that his attitude toward custom and law compromises him with the established order (2:23–3:6, 7:1–15, 10:1–12, 23–25, 42–45). They are only too familiar with his attitude toward those who claim God on their side in order to dominate the people (11:15–19, 12:1–12).

The discussion will scarcely be about a simple rule of behavior. It will be a matter of getting Jesus to admit to any messianic pretensions he may have, to clarify what sort they are, and to betray the consequences they would have for political practice. The Jews thought their subjection to foreign domination would end when the Messiah came. He would drive the Romans out and establish Israel as a great power (Minette de Tillesse 1968, 153).

Worship of king or emperor was a common practice in the Middle East of Jesus' time. It was a mighty bulwark of the established order. Its purpose was to guarantee the concord of the divine and civil orders (Hansen 1973, 144). The idealized effigies minted on coins provided the central authority with an omnipresent and efficacious means of disseminating and reinforcing the notion of sacred royalty (Hansen 1973, 150).

Worship of the emperor had been inaugurated in the Roman Empire during the reign of Augustus. The emperor was addressed as "Savior of the World." Emperor worship had a key political function: it created an important bond, an imperial unity. It was the expression of membership in the empire, of belief in the eternity of the empire (Hansen 1973, 157). The reigning dynasty was referred to as the "household of the gods," the *domus divina*.

The coins in circulation at the time of Jesus portrayed the emperor Tiberius as possessing divine traits and divine titles. It goes without saying that acceptance of the emperor as divine helped preclude rebellion and insubordination. Just as evidently, this ideology stood in total contradiction to faith in the God of Moses and the prophets.

At the other end of the political spectrum from the collaborationists we find the Zealots. For members of this Galilean movement, the payment of the tax in question was plain apostasy. The Zealots saw Israel as God's private property, and consequently no manner of foreign domination could be tolerated. Foreign domination was to be wiped out. Any and every opportunity was to be seized to deliver the promised land, the country God had given Israel, from all profanation and impurity. And so the Zealots went about assassinating collaborationists, members of the priestly familes they considered impure, men married to gentile women, anyone who seemed to them to have violated the temple. They circumcised by force if necessary, under pain of death, every man who lived in Palestine. For the Zealots, anyone who spilled atheist blood was offering sacrifice to God (Hengel 1971, 13). They dreamed of a great Jewish kingdom (Hengel 1971, 64). Indeed, one Simon ben Giora proclaimed the liberation of all Jewish slaves, but not of gentile slaves (Josephus, *The Jewish War* 4:3 [1928], 150–53).

The Zealots fomented hatred. They encouraged a spirit of apocalypse and catastrophe. Torn by internal rivalries, they yet managed to influence the people by taking advantage of their need (Leipoldt and Grundmann 1973, 1:303). There is no likelihood whatever that Jesus was a Zealot. Had he been one, the kingdom of God he announced would have been the kingdom of a chosen few, and this was scarcely his message—quite the contrary. If it had been his message, his execution would have been fully justified by the laws of the empire.

"To God What Is God's"

Jesus does not reply, "Yes, pay the tax to Caesar." Instead he replies: "Give to Caesar what is Caesar's, but give to God what is God's." This is an incisive statement, but as a precise norm it is incomplete—the audience has to complete it. This is the interesting thing about the discussion that preceded the statement. Jesus' adversaries have to help answer the question they have asked (Tannehill 1975, 172). Then comes Jesus' answer—brief, sharp, and forceful. No arguments are brought forward. With one stroke, Jesus changes the whole perspective of the question.

Jesus' reply consists of two parts. The whole passage is constructed in such a way as to point toward this climactic reply. And the "climax of the climax," as we might call it, is the second part of the reply, since it falls in the emphatic, concluding position: "Give to God what is God's" (Tannehill 1975, 173). By placing the names of Caesar and God in such pithy, and parallel, phrases, Jesus prevents us from considering either in isolation (Tannehill 1975, 174).

What is so unexpected, what arrests the attention and receives the emphasis, is the second part of the reply. All the talk has been about duties to Caesar. Very little has been said about God. Then a sudden twist throws the audience off balance. It is the second part of Jesus' reply, precisely, that stamps it as original. Are Jesus' adversaries the people who pretend to be so concerned about the honor due to God? Then why do they overlook, most high-handedly and casually, the fact that this God of theirs ought to constitute the center of this discussion? (Schlier 1970, 265). The basic problem is God and human beings' relationship with God. Jesus demands a return to Caesar of what is Caesar's. But this Caesar surely has nothing at all alongside of and by comparison with what God has. It is in the light of what God is that what belongs to Caesar has to be determined.

First, God's vineyard, that is, his plundered people (Mk 12:1–12) must be restored to him. Then the temple—symbol of a religion profaned by its bonds with commercialism (11:15-18)—and woman (as man's companion and not his slave [10:1-9]) must be "given back to God." One's obligations toward the helpless, whom a disloyal religion has trampled underfoot, thereby rendering itself idolatrous (7:1-15)—this too must be given back. Finally, law must be restored to the complete service of those who are hungering and in need (2:23-16).

The power of God—a power of resurrection, a death-destroying power (Mk 12:18-27)—may not be allowed to be subordinated to the power of those who trample and destroy human beings. God is the absolute, and the emperor is not God. We cannot put God and Caesar on the same level. My obligations to Caesar, if any, must be judged by the yardstick of my commitment to God. God is a power diametrically opposed to the power of money (Mt 6:24); Caesar's power is the appurtenance of money. Total commitment to God demands that I love my neighbor as myself (Mk 12:28-34); Caesar's lordship is an exploitative and enslaving power. (This draws our attention to one more interesting thing in this discussion about paying a tax to Caesar. Jesus carries no money!)

Commitment to God delivers us from body-and-soul commitment to any power that deifies a few and disfigures or destroys the majority. Accordingly, this text may not be treated as a pretext for washing our hands of politics. Rather it is an urgent invitation to live the freedom of the daughters and sons of God. The God of Jesus Christ is not in the service of the gods of this world. He is the demand for universal equality, for a communion of sisters and brothers everywhere.

BEHIND THE MASK OF HOLINESS

Front Seats in the Synagogue

Jesus ends his activity in Galilee with a powerful criticism of a group of Pharisees and certain scribes or lawyers who had come up from Jerusalem. Their lives were inconsistent, as was their interpretation of scripture. They behaved as if holy scripture itself exonerated them from any responsibility for the material needs of their neighbor. Jesus considered a divorce between honor to God and honor to one's neighbor as total disobedience to God. It was hypocrisy and vile idolatry (Mk 7:6-8, 9-13). At the end of his Galilean activity, Jesus also warns his disciples against the influence of the Pharisees, who have closed themselves to God and who demand that God be like them (Mk 8:15; cf. 8:11-13, 3:1-6). Jesus' public activity comes to an end in Jerusalem, where he warns one and all against the behavior of the scribes, the lawyers (12:38-40), who have already been challenged by his teaching before the whole people (12:35-37).

Jesus began his days in Jerusalem by teaching (Mk 11:17). He does the same as these days draw to a close (12:35-40). Both times he attacks the behavior of the religious authorities (11:17, 12:38-40), who have sought to make use of God. This is something which Jesus simply cannot abide. Jesus' life is the diametrical opposite of that of the religious authorities. This is what is at stake in the mighty conflict between Jesus and the lawyers: either one seeks to make use of God, and thus tear one's neighbor limb from limb, or one devotes oneself completely to God, and therefore completely to one's neighbor. This is what creates the gaping chasm between Jesus and the lawyers (Mk 1:22, 12:13-17, 28-34, 35-37). This is what arouses in the lawyers their obsession with having Jesus killed (12:12, 11:18, 15:10). This is the sum and substance of the enormous difference between Jesus and the lawyers.

These passages provide us with a mere summary of events, as can be seen from the accounts in Matthew (23:1-36) and Luke (11:37-54). One is struck by the similarities between Mark 12:39 and Luke 11:43, to be sure, but one is also struck by the differences. In Mark, it is the conduct of third parties that is condemned; in Luke, woe is pronounced directly upon those to whom it applies. In Mark, it is the lawyers who are condemned; in Luke it is the Pharisees.

Mark 12:38 repeats what has already been said in verse 35: Jesus is teaching. The purpose of the observation is to underscore the tight bond between the lawyers' teaching and their conduct, their lives. We are to understand that no one who accepts Jesus' teaching can live as these religious and spiritual leaders live.

All this suggests that Mark is adapting an already existing text to the exigencies of his community and his understanding of Jesus. There is nothing to correspond to Mark 12:40 in its parallels, Matthew 23:6 and Luke 11:43. Further, there is a marked grammatical breach between this verse and those preceding. (A literal translation would be : "Be careful of the lawyers . . . Those who devour . . . "—instead of grammar one might expect, such as, "Be careful of the lawyers . . . who devour," or, "Be careful of those who devour. . . .") This further strengthens the impression of a summary.

Jesus criticizes the lawyers' pretensions to a unique place in society. The *agorai* (the public squares—*en tais agorais*, "in public," Mark writes), the synagogues, and banquets are the centers and the symbols of the social life of the time. The lawyers sought to be esteemed as of greater value than all others; they sought to hold a privileged place in society. Their showy dress—the *stolai*—which Jesus criticizes, was probably affected in order to create an impression, a way of making the people think that the lawyers were observing the sabbath in a special manner ("Die *Stolai*" 1963, 383–404). The sabbath was a day of joy, celebrated not only by service in the synagogues, but frequently by banquets as well. It was on the sabbath, the day consecrated to the Lord, that the lawyers sought marks of respect (Windisch 1964–76, 1:496–502). They took special places of honor in the synagogues, where they could be seen by all and could teach to the assembly (Strack and Billerback 1922–28, 1:915). At banquets they tried to arrange to be seated in the places reserved for the most distinguished guests. They sought to have all society revolve around them. They tried to have everything arranged in such a way that all would believe that they deserved the dignity as the solitary channels of truth (Wilckens 1964–76, 7:687–91). The scribes take the day specially dedicated to the honor of God and devote it to their own honor instead. They exchange the honor of God for the glory of their caste. In reality their god is the honor of their privileged caste. John (5:44) takes up the same theme—but in his own way. He places this reproach in Jesus' mouth: "How can people like you believe, when you accept praise from one another yet do not seek the glory that comes from the One [God]?"

Devouring the Savings of Widows

Devouring the savings of widows is a dishonor to God that is translated into dishonor to one's neighbor. The scribes wipe out means of subsistence of helpless folk, as widows were in the society of the time. They destroy those they were supposed to defend. They take advantage of the helplessness of widows to augment their power. Their charade of piety has managed to have the administration and legal defense of widows' inheritances entrusted to them (Darrett 1972, 1-9). In assaulting the right of these people who were socially so weak, they are assaulting the very cause of God (Ex 22:22; Is 1:17, 23, 10:2). These self-styled experts on God, these reputed knowers of God's will, are in practice God's enemies. By their deeds they have incurred a severe sentence before the judgment seat of God (Wis 6:6).

Remain the Last One of All

Jesus energetically rejected the formation of castes or anything else that might encourage ambition for power on the part of his disciples. The one who wishes to be first must be the last of all, the servant of all (Mk 9:35). This is the only greatness Jesus acknowledges. For him, all other "greatness" is oppression and tyranny (Mk 10:42-45). He himself, entering Jerusalem as a king, enters it as a lowly and poor man (11:1-10).

Those who do not place all their goods at the service of the poor cannot be Jesus' disciples (Mk 10:21). Jesus sends his disciples forth to proclaim the reign of God by using only humble means of spreading the truth (6:6-13). The disciples honor Jesus and his Father who has sent him by demonstrating the greatest respect and generosity toward the least significant of persons (9:36-37). Jesus himself spreads for the poor the banquet of hope, without their having to pay a single penny (6:36-44). Love of God with one's whole heart necessarily issues in a society of brothers and sisters, a society of equals.

Chapter 5

The Way of the Cross

LET'S TALK ABOUT A MURDER

During the years of the First "World" War, Martin Dibelius described the Gospel of Mark as "an account of the Passion with a long prologue." Indeed not only does the entire last third of Mark's Gospel tell of the Passion and death of Jesus, but as early as chapter 3 we learn of the intent to murder Jesus. The theme recurs throughout the whole Gospel.

We usually speak simply of Jesus' "death." Properly speaking, we should refer to his murder, his assassination. The Pharisees plotted with the Herodians to do away with Jesus (Mk 3:6). At one point Jesus went to Phoenicia and hoped to pass unnoticed there (7:24). Jesus said he would be killed (9:31). The chief priests and the lawyers sought to do away with him (11:18, 12:12). They personally went about seeking a way of putting him to death by treachery (14:1), and indeed they did find a traitor (14:10–11).

THE AGONY

Once the supper with his disciples was over, Jesus was active no longer. He healed no more; he preached no more; he held no more discussions with the lawyers and potentates. He lost all freedom of movement and initiative. All that awaited him now was treachery, abandonment, slander, hatred, intrigue, torture, rejection, derision, and death.

Gradually Jesus is reduced to an object. It is his great test and trial. He is swept along toward catastrophe. Nothing will be left to him; the people no longer respond to him; the authorities gloat at his torture; his disciples abandon him and disappear instead of proclaiming the kingdom of God. He had wanted to form a community, and now his friends scatter. Jesus is the blighted grain of wheat that falls to the earth and dies, failing to produce the fruit of the kingdom. He will be led forth and presented to the people as the false prophet, an enemy of God, a defilement. Jesus is alone, without consolation or life. He is totally unarmed in the face of the death prepared for him by the wickedness of human beings.

Jesus feels the test literally in his flesh, as a burden crushing him, beating him to earth. Jesus does not want death. He wants life. His confusion is complete. He feels unhinged, as he has made those around him feel before and as he is to make them feel once more—*thambeisthai, ekthambeisthai*. Everything collapses and his followers are faced with the inconceivable (Mk 1:27, 10:24), with a baffling wonder, (10:32), with sheer terror (16:5–6).

Jesus feels his whole being caught up in turbulence. He contemplates the treachery he is about to suffer (Jn 13:21) and the manner of death awaiting him (Jn 12:27). Until now he has been everyone's mainstay; now he has to beg the encouragement of a few disciples. The pain of it causes him to fall face first to the ground (Vanhoye 1971, 384). Jesus wishes he could die before all this happens. Jesus would prefer death now, failed prophet that he is (Jon 4:9)—the prophet who sees all roads blocked (1 Kgs 19:4).

Unlike Jonah, Jesus prays. Unlike Elijah, he does not make his own heart's desire the center of his prayer. Jesus has always prayed at the decisive moments of his life—at the beginning of his public activity in Galilee (Mk 1:35) as at its climactic conclusion (6:46)—and so we scarcely need be astonished that Jesus prays at the beginning of his great suffering, the beginning of the end of his life. Prayer to Jesus is the key to being able to face uncertainty and pain. Here in his agony, it is the solitary means of withstanding this trial. Only with prayer can Jesus remain at one with God, come what may. Prayer is at the very heart of the Gethsemane scene (Mk 14:32, 35–36, 39), but this prayer is a struggle.

Jesus de-solemnizes God in his prayer. He speaks to God in absolute familiarity. God is utterly close to Jesus. For him, no one is closer than God. God is his *Abba*, his "papa." You can tell God anything, and he will understand everything. Prayer for Jesus is an expression of trust in God and tenderness for God. Jesus can only express his relationship with God by this absolute simplicity. The God Jesus addresses can only be the God of the impossible (Mk 10:27, 11:23–24). Even when he is strapped down powerless himself, Jesus is fully convinced that with God all things are possible (14:38). Even in an absolute dead end, a no-exit situation, what is most important to Jesus is that the divine will be done. The draught that awaits him—the *potērion*, "the cup"—is bitter indeed, but it is God who has decided upon it for Jesus (10:38; cf. Pss 16:5, 23:5). Jesus does not want it, surely, but much less does he want to be at odds with God his Father (Mk 14:36). After all, the single concern of his whole life has been the realization of God's will to justice and reconciliation (Mt 6:9–13; 8:25).

In reply to Jesus' prayer, the traitor and the soldiers arrive (14:41). Jesus has received no consolation. What he has received is the strength to face the difficult, final trial (14:42). Jesus meets his Father across the cup held out to him, which he would have wished taken away (León-Dufour 1979).

The first Christians described this struggle of Jesus in the same terms the psalms use to express the tension, the struggles, of the just person who suffers (Pss 42:6, 10, 12; 43:2–5; 31:10), the innocent one exposed to the assaults of the impious and the unjust (Ps 71:4, 10; 36:12; 37:32). For the first Christians, it is in this suffering and death (14:36; 15:39) more than in the transfiguration that Jesus is revealed for who he really is (Gnilka 1978, 2:294). He is the Son of God, in whom God's will becomes transparent for us. He is the human being in total concord with God. Nothing, not the most resounding failure, not the most humiliating death, can separate him from God. In him is revealed how God comes near us human beings who must suffer and die.

When Mark wrote his Gospel, Christians were in a most difficult pass. They were hated and persecuted for their faith (Mk 13:9–13), and on this account many fell away (4:17). Many were unprepared to face their predicament.

Neither were Jesus' first disciples prepared (Mk 8:32, 9:32). The three disciples who witnessed Jesus' first cure (1:29–31) and his power over death (5:27–43), who saw manifested in him God's nearness and transparent goodness (9:2-9), and for whom Jesus deciphered the web of history (13:1-8) understand nothing of what Jesus is or what he seeks, just as in the transfiguration (9:6). They are blind to his message (14:40). Like the blind Bartimaeus (10:46-52), they need to be healed before they can see to follow in the footsteps of the Master. The dullness and incompetence of the disciples is a matter of record (Mk 14:37-38, 40-41). They are like the servants surprised at their lord's return (13:36)—their hope has numbed, and they have lost their strength.

In order to be able to face this unlooked-for trial (Mk 14:38), one must keep alert and awake in the Lord's service (13:33-37). Persevering hope is a deep, hard struggle, and one which cannot be won without prayer (14:38). Only through prayer will Jesus' struggle cease to be a matter of indifference to us, something that happened long ago and far away.

The disciples' sleep—so insisted upon in Mark's Gospel—is not so much something they do, something in *their* biography, as it is an urgent invitation to the Christian community to be ready to face the same struggle—Jesus' struggle—and to bear him witness in the midst of one's own great weakness—to bear witness to the saving power of God.

THE ARREST

Jesus' word is cut short by those who want to abort his praxis. Judas, one of the Twelve, is head of the death squad (Mk 14:43). Power has need of treachery in order to overpower Jesus. Violence predominates all through the scene. The word repeated again and again is *kratein* or *sullabein*, "arrest" or "lay hands on" (14:44 [twice], 46, 48, 49, 51). Only two individuals are mentioned by name—Jesus, the innocent victim, and Judas, the instrument of repressive power (14:10-11). The mighty seek to overpower Jesus by trickery (14:1). The gladness of Passover is blurred by the specter of Judas' betrayal (14:12-26).

It would seem that Jesus is being "arrested" by a hired gang (Taylor 1966, 538). At the instance of the chief priests, the scribes or lawyers, and the elders or senators, Jesus is approached by a motley rabble armed with swords and clubs with a traitor at their head (Mk 14:43). These are the tools of power: blows and treachery. Jesus is arrested by the chief priests, the lawyers, and the large landowners. The position of High Priest was the monopoly of four families. For all practical purposes in Jesus' time the position had been "cornered" by the house of Annas. Scripture scholar Martin Hengel tells us that five sons of Annas had attained to the dignity of High Priest, and that they profited from their position and enriched themselves through the commerce in animals needed for sacrifice. They bought the good will of the Roman procurators with lavish bribes, and the procurators, in turn, used this priestly aristocracy as their intermediary in dealing with the Jewish people (Hengel 1973b, 36–37).

The chief priests in Jesus' time were created and dismissed at the whim of the sovereign. Twenty-eight High Priests between 37 B.C. and A.D. 70 were chosen from among the various priestly families. The members of the families who supplied the High Priest constituted a priestly aristocracy, the group of chief-priests-in-the-plural who appear so frequently in the New Testament (de Vaux 1967, 2:274).

The upper echelon of Palestine's aristocracy was made up primarily of the priestly nobility and the members of the High Priest's family. They gained their income from the temple treasury, from their lands, from temple commerce and from the appointment of relatives to the administrative magistratures (Leipoldt and Grundmann 1973, 1:201).

Their customs and mores were not very different from the Hellenist magnates. They were extremely conservative—they were Sadducees (Leipoldt and Grundmann 1973 1:281). Specifically, Caiaphas collaborated with Pontius Pilate by way of a tacit understanding. They were on good terms, to their mutual advantage. Pilate was the protégé of Sejanus, the most powerful person in Rome, one of the ringleaders of the anti-Jewish movement there (Leipoldt and Grundmann 1973, 1:179). The lawyers were the ideological power—the prestigious interpreters of the Law.

The disciples' lack of faith grows by leaps and bounds. Those closest to Jesus show total insensitivity to his presentiment of death, and one of them, Judas, an intended pillar of the new people Jesus meant to create, is transformed into the indispensable instrument of his murder.

The authorities seek to avoid any difficulties that might interfere with Jesus' arrest (Mk 14:1). Judas smoothes the way. The band of soldiers had not known where Jesus was to spend the evening, nor could they tell which one he was in the dark as easily as could one of his disciples. Judas converts the sign of friendship into notice of death (14:44). Friendship and veneration, symbolized by the kiss of honor bestowed upon a master and teacher, now are trampled underfoot (14:45). Judas himself gives the orders to grasp Jesus and hold him fast as if he were a dangerous beast (14:44).

Now the cataclysm of the violence erupts around Jesus. One of those present strikes and mutilates someone in the employ of the High Priest (14:47). (The text in no way indicates that it was one of Jesus' disciples who did so. It was simply a "bystander, someone" *parestēkōs,* just as in 14:69–70, 15:35, 39 [Schneider n.d., 201]).

Jesus has behaved as a teacher, a spiritual master. They treat him like a bandit (14:48). He taught by light of day. They assault him by night. He has nothing to hide. By contrast, the mighty have need of darkness to carry out their plans. They cannot make Jesus hold his tongue by arguments (11:33, 12:17, 24–27, 34), they can silence him with blows (14:48, 65).

Judas has turned traitor. Jesus is silent. The words he addresses to the band of soldiers are the only ones with which he defends himself throughout the whole course of the Passion. His silence makes it perfectly clear that he may not allow himself any defense that takes up the arms of the enemy.

Once Jesus is arrested, all his disciples desert him (Mk 14:50). His solitude, his loneliness and abandonment, is precisely that of the poor person who trusts in God instead of power or money (Pss 31:12, 37:14–15, 38:12; 41:10; Jer 37:11–16). His disciples leave him when he is most in need.

"Deserting" Jesus (*aphentes auton*—[Mk 14:50]) is the contrary of "following" him (*akolouthein*). Compare the use of the two verbs in Mark 10:28–29. This desertion of Jesus is a renunciation of the status of discipleship (Schneider n.d., 205). For the disciples, to follow a prisoner is an intrinsic contradiction, automatic insanity (209). They do not believe it worth running any risk for a poor defenseless whipping-boy. Not only is Jesus no longer of any interest to anyone, but his erstwhile friends prefer embarrassment and ridicule to having to suffer anything for him (Mk 14:51). All this violence and cowardice will, in the end, serve God's salvation plan for human beings.

THE TRIAL

Certain words leap out at us from the description of the scene of Jesus before the Sanhedrin: *testimony* and its cognates (Mk 14:55, 56 [twice], 57, 59, 60, 63), *silent* (14:61; cf. 14:60, and the great silence of 14:65), and *death*, which opens and closes the scene (vv 55, 64), providing the whole with a framework by what the classical rhetoricians call "inclusion." So we are not surprised when we find that we are assisting at a scene of testimony and death.

As before, we see striking contrasts. Some scholars rightly see a triptych here composed of (1) an introduction (Mk 14:53–54); (2) the trial (14:55–56); and (3) Peter's denial (14:66–72). In view of the continuity and thematic affinity of the two scenes—the trial and the denial—neither can be interpreted except in relationship to the other.

False testimony against Jesus abounds. Not only is the testimony false, it is self-contradictory (14:56, 59). No "evidence" is reported to us other than that someone alleges to have heard Jesus say, "I will destroy this temple made by human hands," and "In three days I will construct another not made by human hands" (14:58). This testimony is artificially manufactured in order to procure the death sentence (v 55), and because it is contradictory, it should have no legal weight (vv 56, 59). But legality is dead. The defenders of the Law have taken upon themselves the responsibility of abolishing the Law.

During the testimony and the High Priest's interrogation, Jesus of Nazareth utters not a solitary syllable. He is silent, as he was silent at Judas' treacherous word and as he will be silent before the questionable "honesty" of Pontius Pilate (Mk 15:4–5).

Jesus—reduced to an object—is now brought before the representatives of wisdom, prosperity, and holiness (Mk 14:53). These great ones have no concern for anything but his death and whatever false testimony may provide them with a pretext for it (14:55–59). It is useless to speak to such as these (cf. Lk 22:67–68). Jesus' silence is the silence of the just, of the suffering innocent. By his silence he unmasks the hollowness of power. Sounding in the background of Mark 14:61 is this passage from Isaiah:

> Though he was harshly treated, he submitted
>   And opened not his mouth;
> Like a lamb led to the slaughter
>   or a sheep before the shearers,
>   he was silent and opened not his mouth [Is 53:7].

And behind Mark 14:65:

> He opens my ear that I may hear;
> And I have not rebelled,
>   I have not turned back [Is 50:4–5].

In all the other controversies, Jesus closed his adversaries' mouths. If they were unwilling to understand his works and his words then, it would certainly be superfluous to defend them now. The judges whom the free and liberating truth had struck dumb (Mk 3:1–6, 11:27–33), now demand that Jesus speak. Once they fell silent before truth and life; now Jesus falls silent before deceit and crime. Jesus is the suffering Just One (Ps 38:12–16). But here is not just any Just One. Here is the Servant of the Lord, who suffers in order to win redemption for all (Servant Songs of Second Isaiah).

The accusation lodged against Jesus contains its particle of truth, but his adversaries are using truth in order to deceive. Stephen will be accused of saying "that Jesus the Nazarene will destroy this place and change the customs which Moses handed down to us" (Acts 6:14), and in John 2:19 we find similar words placed in Jesus' mouth. Indeed, while he had not said that he would destroy the temple, he most certainly had said that the temple and what it meant would pass away (Mk 13:1–2).

The temple was not only the religious center of the Jewish world, it was also the economic center of Judea. Artisans, spice merchants and their collaborators, construction workers, incense manufacturers, money-changers or bankers—all lived principally by the temple. The temple was Jerusalem's principal source of work. Temple worship was the focal point of all business and trade. All Jews, even if they lived abroad, were under obligation to pay the temple tax of two drachmas (7.2 grams of silver). And the temple was flooded with free-will offerings besides.

Jerusalem's population of some fifty-five thousand was more than doubled at Passover time when pilgrims came. Pilgrims were obliged to tithe a second time (Jeremias 1977, 101). These contributions enabled Judea to balance its trade deficit. The entire temple treasury was controlled by the priestly aristocracy. In addition, the revenue from the licensing of commercial installations in the temple's outer court was the perquisite of the High Priest (Leipoldt and Grundmann 1973, 1:199).

For all who dominated the people or influenced their ideas, the temple, the seat of economic power, was the place where God met the people of Israel. But Jesus dissociated God from money and repression. For Jesus, the place of encounter with God is elsewhere. The way to approach God is different. The people have another center. These privileged avenues are not in things but in human bodies. The temple, that warranty for the security and order of an asymmetrical society, a society of unequals, no longer has any reason to exist that Jesus can see. For Jesus, the point of God's encounter with human beings bears no resemblance to a den of thieves, and it has nothing to do with exclusivisms of any kind (Mk 10:17). Jesus maintains the primacy of prophecy over legalism. God relates to human beings; God is not shackled to things.

To the temple that is the work of human beings, Jesus contrasts a temple which is not the work of human beings. To the temple that must necessarily pass away, Jesus opposes a temple that will never grow old. Over against the deeds of human beings, Jesus places the plan of God (as in Mk 7). To hypocrisy and oppression, Jesus contrasts fidelity and love (Mk 2, 3, 7). This is another sort of worship, surely, a totally different view of God.

By driving the entrepreneurs from the temple, Jesus is making a clear statement as to what he is "after." Instead of a den of thieves, Jesus wants a temple that is a house of prayer for all peoples (Mk 11:17). He wants a religion divorced from all oppression and exclusivism. Jesus is reliving the battle and tradition of the prophets. Jeremiah struggled fiercely against a smug, hypocritical religion, a religion concerned with things instead of with the exploited human being, a religion that sought to take advantage of God. In his struggle he proclaimed the oracle of the Lord:

Reform your ways and your deeds, so that I may remain with you in this place. . . . Only . . . if you no longer oppress the resident alien, the orphan, and the widow; if you no longer shed innocent blood in this place . . . will I remain with you in this place. . . . But here you are, putting your trust in deceitful words to your own loss! Are you to steal and murder, commit adultery and perjury, burn incense to Baal, go after strange gods that you know not, and yet come to stand before me in this house which bears my name, and say: "We are safe; we can commit all these abominations again"? [Jer 7:3–10].

For this mighty prophet, a religion which endorses a permanent state of oppression is an abomination. It is idolatry. It is the worship of falsehood and consequently the denial of God. This is Jesus' battle too—only, he is carrying it to hitherto inconceivable extremes.

Jeremiah's adversaries were gentlemen of intense piety—just as Jesus' enemies, in their own way, were proper and beyond reproach. These priests and prophets "laid hold of" Jeremiah and "said to the princes and to all the people, 'This man deserves death; he has prophesied against this city, as you have heard with your own ears' "(Jer 26:8,11). The similarity to Jesus' trial is plain as day. Jesus is the new Jeremiah, power is presented as the enemy of genuine prophecy.

Ezekiel spoke of a new, indestructible sanctuary and a permanent, definitive presence of God with the people (Ez 37:26–28). Once the new temple was erected (Ez 40:4, 42:20), the glory of the Lord would return to inaugurate a new era (43:1–9), one in which "they shall put far from me their harlotry and the corpses of their kings, and I will dwell in their midst forever" (43:9). From the temple, the water of life would flow. It would be like a return to paradise (47:1–12). In proclaiming a "new temple," Jesus declares exclusivism meaningless and senseless. No longer is there any justification for dividing human beings into categories.

Jesus has not struck up another discussion over a point of the Law or introduced one more school of interpretation. Jesus has ushered in a new era, a new life, and has voided all the values maintained and defended by the lords of his time. Over against his claim arises the High Priest's question:

"Are you the Messiah, the Son of the Blessed One?" Then Jesus answered: "I am; and you will see the Son of Man seated at the right hand of the Power and coming with the clouds of heaven" [Mk 14:61–62].

This response comes from a totally Palestinian world. "I am" would normally mean, "Yes, I am the one you mean," in reply to an adjuration as solemn as that of the High Priest in the exercise of his function. If we place ourselves in the position of the High Priest, "I am" coming from Jesus can mean nothing but "Yes, I am the Messiah." And indeed, "Son of God" in the gospels indicates a *mission* (see Mt 4:1–7; Jn 8:38–44, 10:36). Jesus is the one sent, the revealer of divine truth. "Son of God" indicates a special relationship with God. Jesus is called the Son of God both at the beginning and at the end of Mark's Gospel (1:1, 15:39). He has shown us God, he has brought us near God, as no one had even done before.

To be "seated at the right hand of the Almighty" was also said of the king and indicated participation in divine power. The king was looked upon as God's delegate on earth. The king ruled in the name of God, with God's authority and assistance (2 Cor 9:8, 28:5, 29:23).

The "Son of Man coming on the clouds of heaven" was an image from the Book of Daniel (chap. 7). The people of Israel, being persecuted by Antiochus Epiphanes, receive the apocalyptic promise that God will take up their cause and that justice will quickly be done. The chapter describes four beasts corresponding to four oppressive empires. The fourth beast is described as terrible, fearsome, mighty, with great iron teeth for quartering and devouring, and what it did not devour it trampled with its feet (Dn 7:7). But "the beast was slain" (7:11), and the others "lost their dominion" (v 12). By contrast, the Son of Man, coming "on the clouds of heaven . . . received dominion, glory, and kingship. . . . His dominion is an everlasting dominion that shall not be taken away . . . " (vv 13–14). His is real power, imperishable power. This Son of Man represents "the holy ones of the Most High" (vv 18, 22), that is, the people of the Lord, who shall be present when the court is convened and the fourth beast, the terrible one, is judged (v 26).

It is to all this that Jesus answers "Yes." Jesus is conscious of representing the people of saints, of holy ones. Jesus is the head of the people who destroy the power of the beast. Jesus holds himself up as the total contradiction of oppressive power, which is represented by those who condemn him. The beasts of the Book of Daniel rise up out of the abyss (Dn 7:3); they personify the power of evil, the power of destruction. Jesus' reply is a judgment passed on his judges. The one they condemn is the ideal personification of the people, their struggles, their faith, their hope. Jesus has been given the strength and power of God. The judges are handing down a judgment totally at odds with God and are thereby identifying themselves with the "destructive beasts."

By weaving two passages together—one from Daniel 7, the other from Psalm 110—Jesus indicates that the Son of Man is a particular concrete individual, and that he is reigning with God, not only on the terrestrial plane but on the heavenly one as well (Lamarche 1966, 147-63). The dovetailing of these two passages reveals that Mark sees in Jesus more than a simple Messiah.

Jesus' answer contains the word *opsesthe*, "you will see." In the Bible this is a verb of revelation (Ex 16:7; Mi 7:16). It indicates a living, vital experience (Is 40:5, 52:10) (Vanhoye 1970, 85). When Daniel had his vision, the people were suffering and glory was still to come. Jesus stresses his enthronement, the sign of his triumph, just when everything speaks of his annihilation. In repeating this prophecy, Jesus is proclaiming his limitless confidence in God at the very moment when the powers seem to give the lie to any faithfulness on God's part.

Jesus declares his identity and is not understood. This is the only place in Mark's Gospel where all three great messianic titles occur together (Vanhoye 1970, 361). Throughout this Gospel, Jesus has refused to declare openly what he is. But from this moment forward there is no doubt. He is the Messiah, but crushed, slandered, condemned, and ridiculed. He is the Son of God, but betrayed and abandoned. He is the Son of Man, to be tortured and killed. He is the contradiction of everything his interrogators believe in and hope for.

The three powers—political, economic, and religious—condemn Jesus for being a Messiah who is poor and persecuted (Mk 6-7), the enemy of all exploitation (10-12), the liberator of the marginalized and oppressed (1-3), the destroyer of exclusivisms and thereby the joy of the outcast (2:15-16), the one totally uninterested in money (10:17-31, 12:41-44; Mt 5:19-34; Lk 6:20-26), the enemy and unmasker of every type of oppression (Mk 8:14-21, 10:42-45, 12:37-40; Mt 23:1-36; Lk 11:37-53), a Messiah who knows no hatred or greed (Mk 11:25; Lk 6:27-36, 12:13-25), one completely dedicated to service (Mk 10:45; Lk 4:16-22)—a Messiah whose program is abundance for the destitute (Mk 6:30-44; 8:1-13), one completely identified with the exploited and dispossessed (Mt 25:31-46).

With Jesus the kingdom of God has come definitively, and it has come for all. It is a kingdom opposed to the kingdoms that now must crumble (Dt 2:35-43, 5:26-28, 11:4). The rich and powerful are excluded from this kingdom, which triumphs with Jesus (Mk 10:23-24) and is only revealed to little ones, to insignificant persons (10:14-15). In Jesus God is revealed to be on the side of poor and oppressed persons of every kind and the revelation is not given in solemn, complicated words but in altogether concrete deeds. Jesus is a suffering Messiah, but he suffers in order to end suffering. Only through this suffering can the mission of Jesus Christ be understood. It is not to be wondered at, then, that throughout the whole Gospel it is only in Jesus' suffering that his disciples manage to discern his strength and his glory. This knowledge and acceptance are not the fruit of speculation, but the fruit of following the crucified Messiah.

Jesus' trial ends not with a juridical sentence, but with a determination of the "facts of the case": the High Priest pronounces Jesus a blasphemer, an enemy of God (cf. Lv 24:12-16), and rends his garments. The Jewish symbols are sundered, for Jesus is a threat to the Jewish social and religious world.

Jesus is claiming that the glory belonging to the Messiah is now evident as his own. But Jesus' revelation is met with condemnation and blows (Mk 14:65). Jesus has proclaimed that his glory would be seen (14:62); now he has his face covered. He who has been shown to be the new Jeremiah and the fulfillment of the promise of Ezekiel (Mk 14:58) is taunted in a game of "play the prophet." The one who claims to belong to the world of the skies, the power of

God (14:62), is jeered at and spat upon. He who was to come with the power of God (14:62) is welcomed with blows in the face.

PETER'S DENIAL

Jesus' witness (Mk 14:60–62) is full of contrasts with Peter's denial (14:66–72). Jesus gives his testimony in a court of law, before the highest authorities. Peter denies Jesus in a casual encounter with people who have no power at all. As a result of Jesus' testimony he is bound and beaten. Peter denies Jesus when he is at liberty and with no one even spying on him. Jesus has to face false witnesses, the solemn interrogation of the High Priest, and a whole assassination plan. The questions put to Peter are casual ones, a matter of curiosity, or at most of a desire to subject someone to temporary embarrassment. Evidence of Peter's relationship to his Galilean teacher are thrown up to him. Jesus answers more than he is asked concerning his relationship with God. Peter denies more than he is accused of, claiming not even to know what "Jesus" his questioners are talking about. Jesus is completely unknown to him. He who has promised to give his life for Jesus (Mk 14:31) now renounces all contact with him. He who has promised unshakable fidelity even in the midst of universal disloyalty (14:29) is the only one to break off all relations with Jesus and he does so in clear and explicit words. Jesus' dereliction is complete. Even the one who has had the courage to follow him from afar, right into the place where the trial was being held (14:54), denies him when it really counts. After the accusations against him, and his proclamation of his unique relationship with God, nothing awaits Jesus but loneliness, taunts, blows, and God's silence. The cock's crow reminds Peter of what Jesus had foretold (14:30). It keeps him from falling irremediably into temptation. Jesus' forgiveness works efficaciously in the heart of those who have cursed and sworn they know nothing about him (Schilier 1979, 61). When all have abandoned him, and seek to destroy him, Jesus continues to offer his friendship, even to one who turns his back on him. Peter, instead of denying himself (8:34), denies his master (Pesch 1974, 166). But even in desertion and treachery, Jesus does not cease to offer his forgiveness.

In addition to the contrast between Peter and Jesus, we have the contrast between Peter and Judas. Judas takes the initiative, and actively carries out the betrayal (Mk 14:10–14, 43–45); Peter only reacts to inquiries. Judas hands Jesus over to his enemies; Peter merely denies him. Judas betrays Jesus in deeds, Peter only in words. Judas perverts the sign of friendship, placing it at the service of crime. Judas goes looking for Jesus; Peter tries to accompany him. Judas receives money for his treachery; Peter receives nothing. Judas' activity is over once Jesus is betrayed; Peter, remembering Jesus' words, breaks down and weeps (14:72).

The difficulty for Peter, the scandal, consisted in accepting the total presence of God in someone condemned by the machinery of power and exploitation. What is hard for Peter is the contradiction involved, by human standards of judgment, in accepting that God is revealed to us through the suffering of a person who is poor, through a just person being tortured.

With Peter's denial Mark shows us a church of sinners, of cowards and one which is not ashamed to admit it. The church Mark presents to us is a community well aware that it is never safe and secure, not even in its most selfless and disinterested members, and that the only thing it has to rely on is the forgiveness of Jesus Christ. He shows us a church that can switch from denial to repentance thanks only to a Christ crushed and tortured.

Christ grants to this church a partial experience of his own pain and sorrow. The risen Christ gathers together cowards, renegades, and traitors (Mk 16:7) to fill them with the indestructible force of his love.

JESUS BEFORE PILATE

Jesus' trial before Pilate is shown us in a framework marked off by the word *paradidomai*, "handing over" (Mk 15:1, 15). The word (at least in Mark 10:33, 14:11, 18, 21, 41, 42, 44) connotes treachery, disloyalty, unfairness, and even (as in Pss 27:12, 118:21) cruelty.

The principals of the drama are the plenipotentiary representatives of religious power: the High Priests, or Chief Priests. They are entirely bent on Jesus' death (Mk 14:64). For them no bandit or guerrilla is as dangerous as a teacher like Jesus (14:49).

A person of this sort deserves only the instruments of death: treachery (Mk 14:1-2, 10-11, 43-46), mercenary violence (14:43-49), slander (14:55-59), and the accusation of being in league with Satan (14:63-64). Now what has been so long and so carefully in preparation is about to be carried out (15:1; cf. 3:6, 11:18, 12:12, 14:1). Thus the Chief Priests behave like the mercenary guard and the bribed witnesses (15:1, 3-4; cf. 14:43-49, 55-61). To this end, to the purpose of this death, no means—no planning, no repression, no political maneuvering—are spared (15:1). Grave—and false—accusations are lodged against the accused (15:3, 4). The people are incited (15:11). The enmity toward Jesus is mortal here; it is lethal (15:10; cf. Gn 4:5; Ps 2:24). The powers are dedicated heart and soul to the success of their political murder. Their aim is for Jesus to die the most ignominious of deaths and for themselves to continue to occupy the most prestigious positions. Supposedly the defenders of tradition, whose task it is to keep alive the hopes of a people, they hand over a member of that people, a just member, to Pilate, the representative of an oppressive foreign power. And all this they do in the name of God—in the name of their God, religious power. Religious power now shows itself for what it is: the agent of death.

All through his public life, Jesus has shown the religious authorities what it means to seek God anywhere but among the suffering, to seek God far from the exploited. Such a quest is murder and the depths of idolatry. Now these authorities are demonstrating the truth of what they have been told and they are demonstrating it by the way they deal with Jesus. Those who have placed religion in the service of power and money (Mk 12:38-41) now hand over to Caesar what is God's (15:1; cf. 12:13-17).

Mark does not show us a romantic Pilate. He does not seek to exonerate him. Neither all his experience nor the formalities and technicalities of the Law suffice to explain to Pilate what this defendant could possibly be doing here before him (Mk 15:50). But Pilate's decision is not based on fear or ignorance. Without having presided at Jesus' trial, he pronounces him guilty by placing him among those eligible for the Passover amnesty. He even publicly calls him "king of the Jews" (15:9, 12), which will make a verdict of not guilty all the more awkward to hand down. He can see that Jesus is innocent (15:10, 12), yet he allows his freedom to hang on the caprice of the crowd. Instead of behaving as a judge, Pilate turns beggar and pleads for minimal justice (15:14). He does nothing to defend this innocent person from the cruelest and most shameful of deaths. On the contrary, he actually hands him over to this manner of death (15:15). Jesus is nothing to Pilate but another Jew, a poor wretch who has happened to fall into disfavor with the local authorities, for whom Pilate has nothing but contempt.

Pilate does not ask himself whether what the people are demanding is just, not even after seeing their vicious cruelty and hatred. Pilate knows that the religious authorities are behind this whole dirty game, and he knows that they are not to be trusted. He cannot think that they are loyal to the Roman Empire (Blinzler 1969, 306). No, neither the authorities nor the Jewish people have any importance for Pilate. The only important thing for him is not to become entangled, not to get involved—to keep his job. He had been the protégé of Sejanus, the "power behind the throne." But his great patron was liquidated. Now he must move cautiously. He is concerned with his own interests and not those of some poor wretch, even a just and innocent one. The love of power has made Pilate its slave (see 15:14–15), and the type of power enjoyed by Pilate is incapable of saving a just person.

The people have approached the palace, Pilate's residence, not to demand Jesus' death but to beg a crumb of power (Mk 15:8). The people have no interest in doing away with Jesus. They are interested in staying in the good graces of the Chief Priests (15:11), for they are the temple authority, and it is thanks to the temple that the people live better than their rustic Galilean compatriots (Theissen 1978). If Jesus threatened their condition of relative privilege, then do away with him indeed, and with everything having to do with him. As the saying goes, "When the hound dies, the mange goes away." The crowd knows that if it is Barabbas who is to live, the temple will continue to operate.

All who have in any way contributed to Jesus' death have more than enough reason for doing so.

Jesus is snatched from among the people as a malefactor and handed over to the pagans to be killed (Mk 9:31, 10:33). This is what awaits any messenger of God (12:5, 7, 8), any great prophet (6:17, 27). Jesus is bound, hauled from one place to another, "handed over" (15:1), accused (15:3–4), interrogated (15:2–4), held in the open, threatened with death, made to hear cries for his death, used as a plaything, tortured, and sentenced to death (15:9–15). Tortured, Jesus is no longer master of his own body, no longer master of his own life. His life is toyed with (vv 9–15), his body is toyed with (vv 16–20). Jesus is reduced to silence. The one thing he says goes unheeded.

The commentators make much of Jesus' silence. They usually refer to the Psalms of Lamentation. Silence, we are told, is the authentic attitude of the just person who suffers but who still trusts God utterly (Pss 38:14–16, 39:10, 109:4). I do not deny the validity of this explanation. But we should also have an explanation in function of the logic of the Gospel.

The religious leaders had already accused Jesus of blasphemy (Mk 2:6), of violating the sanctity of the sabbath (2:23, 3:5), and of being the instrument of Satan (3:22). These accusations constitute the theological grounds for his execution. Unflaggingly his enemies had sought to undermine his image, to discredit him in the eyes of the people, to destroy his morale. They proclaimed that he dined and made merry with the dregs of society, and that indeed he was in his element there (2:16). They claimed his religion was not strict enough (2:18), and that he made no account of the ritual purity considered to be so necessary for worthy participation in the rites of worship (2:1–5). They sought to make him out as the destroyer of an order they judged to be immutable and divine, in which a woman would always be an object for her husband (10:1–4).

Jesus had already clearly answered all these accusations. Indeed, he had asked his persecutors to make a commitment to the truth, but they had taken refuge in silence (11:27–33). They had not known what to say to Jesus when he showed them that true love for God necessarily comports love for one's neighbor, and that nothing else can replace this type of love (12:28–34; cf. 3:1–5, 7:9–13). Nor had they any answer when Jesus showed them the groundlessness of their hopes (12:35–37; cf. 12:18–27). Now, however, their kind of truth is being expressed—in spittle, jibes, and blows (14:65). Here at last was the local authorities' "truth." They do as the traitor has done and as their mercenaries have done (15:1): they have treated Jesus as if he were an animal, a wild beast, a dangerous criminal (14:45, 15:1). Jesus is no longer a human being for them. Jesus cannot speak to them in a language they are willing to use. And so he keeps silence. Jesus' silence throughout the judicial procedures against him actually serves to unmask the farce.

Pilate would not have been interested in a mere religious delict. So the chief priests accuse Jesus of claiming to be a king, of seeking to be rid of Caesar's dominion. According to Roman law, a judge must pass sentence based on a confession obtained from the accused (see Sallust 1904, 42). Pilate is not convinced that Jesus has confessed to any crime (Mk 15:4–5, 10, 12, 14, 15). So legality has been bungled. Now the famous "imperial justice" will show what it is worth. Behold the coalition of the two powers that hate each other—the religious and the political. In this instance their legality only serves to set the guilty free and slaughter the innocent. They seek nothing but their own interests. God and justice for them are no more than facade and pretext. They must forthwith be rid of anyone who shows them a God intimately united with the suffering. Jesus standing trial is the suffering just one, oppressed by the powerful (Pesch 1974, 156).

The Letter to the Hebrews is not indulging in pious exaggeration when it speaks of the "shame" of the cross (Heb 12:2). Jurist Julius Paulus calls crucifixion the "maximum penalty" (Hengel 1976, 145). Callistratus says the same (Blinzler 1969, 357). For Tacitus it is the punishment of slaves (Tacitus, *Histories* [1952], p. 259). Cicero calls it "the worst extreme of the tortures inflicted upon slaves" (Cicero, *In Verrem* [1935], 655). For Cicero, not only should the cross be done away with as a punishment, it should not be thought of, seen, or heard of. Its very name is unworthy of a Roman citizen, a free person (Cicero, *Pro Rabirio* [1927], 466–69). A passage from Plato's *Republic* is famous for its prophetic description of the lot of one who would be found to be really just:

> The just man who is thought unjust will be scourged, racked, bound—will have his eyes burnt out; and, at last, after suffering every kind of evil, he will be impaled [Book 2, no. 361].

In other words, for Plato too, crucifixion was the worst of torments. In his comedies, Plautus has left us samples of the worst insults used by the lower classes, some of which refer to crucifixion: *cruciarius* or *patibulatus* meant literally "gibbeted on a cross," but was used metaphorically. *Crucis offla* "gallous meat," meant something like "gallous bird," and *in crucem*, or *in malam maximam crucem*, meant something like "Go to hell" (see Plautus, *Asinaria* 940 [1937], 226–27).

The cross, then, was a loathsome reality, which "decent people" did not even mention, but which they approved and judged to be necessary. Cicero, for example, was aghast that Verres would have crucified a Roman citizen, but he thought it well enough that that torture be undergone by slaves. Seneca approved the crucifixion of brigands. One Roman emperor refused to utter the word *crucifixion* but had hundreds of people crucified (Hengel 1976, 148).

The cross, then, in the Roman period was capital punishment for slaves, felons, deserters, and, in the provinces, people of humble condition who had instigated revolts or engaged in banditry (Nieri 1929–39, 12:1). People of a more comfortable station might escape this torture, but the lowly were the victims of every sadism their executioners could invent in connection with it (Seneca, *Of Consolation* 6:20 [1889], 192). Crucifixion was the capital punishment imposed for crimes of high treason (Justinian, *Digest* 38:2; 48:19). It was the ideal instrument for the maintenance of the Pax Romana, which was based on exploitation and slavery (Blinzler 1969, 358). In the Greek world, crucifixion was a familiar mode of execution for slaves and peasants (Hengel 1976, 173).

Among the Jews, crucifixion was a punishment reserved to traitors, those who had cursed the people or otherwise sinned directly against them (*Temple Roll* 64:6–10), and those who had denied God by engaging in idolatrous orgies (*Targumim Neofiti,* and Pseudo-Jonathan, on Numbers 25:4). Victims of crucifixion were considered to be "cursed by God and man" a blotch on the land (*Temple Roll* 64:13; Dt 21:23).

Throughout the Mediterranean Basin, then, crucifixion was socially and ethically shameful. The victim was a political delinquent, sentenced for disturbing the peace, the order, the authorities, and the ideals of this world. That the dishonor might be complete, burial was generally denied.

So we see that Jesus' sentence places him among the proverbial "wicked" (Is 53:12). This was done to Jesus by the persons who were the most religious, the persons best schooled in the scriptures, the finest scholars of their time—the great ones of religion and economics. This was done to Jesus by political power and by a people blinded by their immediate, exclusive interests. The primitive Christian community was suffering this same rejection when Mark wrote his Gospel.

Pilate handed Jesus over to be scourged (Mk 15:15) before being crucified. Scourging was the standard preliminary to execution by crucifixion. There was no limit as to how hard or how long a victim might be beaten. His blood flowed in rivers, and loathsome abcesses formed on his hands and feet. His flesh hung from his bones in chunks. Often enough his entrails were laid bare (Josephus, *Jewish War* 2:5 [1928], 538–59). The purpose of the scourging was to place the victim on display in the most demeaning possible way (Blinzler 1969, 321).

Next Jesus was mocked. He was stripped naked, and a scarlet robe was hung about his torn shoulders (15:17). After all, he had said he was a king. He was given a crown, but it was a crown of thorns (15:18). Then he was hailed as king indeed (15:18), with religious homage such as Eastern potentates were accustomed to receive (15:19). The whole palace guard was called together to join in the amusement (15:16).

We may gather from certain details that all this was not just good, clean fun. The crown was made of thorns (v 18). The one being mocked was a prisoner who had been sentenced to death, scourged (v 15), and spat on (v 19)—this last action was a sign of profound contempt, then as now (Dt 25:9; Is 50:66; Jb 30:10). Jesus' head was hit repeatedly with a reed (Mk 15:19). Only after this bloody carnival was he dragged from the governor's residence to be crucified (15:20). By this time Jesus was so debilitated that he was unable to carry the crossbar from which he was sentenced to hang (15:21).

Historical parallels have been sought to give the literary genre of our description a clearer definition. The very search is indicative of the pedantry into which the specialists have fallen. Surely it should suffice to recall that (1) the soldiery had been recruited among Palestinian gentiles who saw in the Jews a threat to their own survival and so detested them with a hatred that was truly deadly; (2) the condemned person represented a danger to the institutions the soldiers defended and which in turn supported them; (3) unjust regimes do not recruit their death squads from among the most fastidious or psychologically best adjusted; and (4) torture has always been much the same, so we really need not look to history to learn how it is done. Yet scholars continue to look to ancient history.

Jesus is silent throughout (see Pss 38:14, 39:10). Object of mockery that he is in this scene, he recalls for us the situation of the "just one" of the psalms. Jesus' suffering is the suffering of the just one, the person who trusts in God, the defender of the weak and exploited (Pss 35:10, 15-16, 31:12, 39:9, 44:14, 69:8, 19-20). And so the first Christians, hearing Mark, were able to identify the cause of the afflictions they themselves were suffering, especially at the hands of the powerful.

Mark probably wrote his Gospel in Rome, or at least in some place dominated by Rome, during a period when the empire was deified, both in its structure and in the person of the emperor. He wrote it at a time when Christians enjoyed no official regard, and when their general popularity was at a low ebb.

And so, inspired and encouraged by my faith—for if my beliefs were the same as those of the Mafia or a political gang or an economic consortium, then I would not do this—I invite my brothers and sisters in the faith to join me in seriously wondering whether we are not too much like Pilate, or the Chief Priests, or a brutal people.

Chapter 6

And They Crucified Him

THE CRUCIFIED ONE

Jesus was hauled away from the governor's residence and out of the city to be crucified. A blasphemer (Lv 24:14), or one who broke the sabbath (Nm 15:35–36)—in other words, one who had sinned gravely against the holiness of God—was to be completely torn away from the community. Such a one was like manure, to be cast as far from the house as possible and gotten out of sight as quickly as possible. The custom of inflicting punishment outside the city walls was known in Rome, too (Plautus, *Miles Gloriosus* 359 [1930], 160–61). Because Jesus was too weak to carry his cross, "a man named Simon of Cyrene" (Mk 15:21) was pressed into service.

The thematic root that keeps pounding our ears like the sound of a hammer (Vss 21–32) is "cross" and its cognates. Mark's purpose is to bring us to realize how degrading a death Jesus is suffering. But no detailed description of the crucifixion is given. It was unnecessary. Nor was it something the poor and the other marginalized really liked to hear about. No, they knew all about crucifixions.

After so many tortures the prisoner had nails driven through his wrists so that his arms could be spread wide and nailed to the crossbar. Another nail was driven through the heel-bones of both feet, with one foot atop the other. A wood chip was fixed to the head of this nail, to help hold the nailed feet tight.

Generally a kind of board was placed under the buttocks so that

102

the prisoner could somehow sit against it. This helped prevent the hands and feet from tearing away, after all the work to attach them, and served to prolong the agony (Martini 1971, 494ff.; Charlesworth 1972–73, 149ff.; Strack and Billerbeck 1922–28, 1:1037). Upon his arrival at the place of torment, Jesus refused the myrrhed wine offered to dull the pain of those undergoing capital punishment.

The executioners divided the prisoner's clothes among them. (Mk 15:24) (Strack and Billerbeck 1922–28, 1:1038; Blinzler 1969, 369). Numerous commentators see a clear reference here to Psalm 22:18. But curiously if the Passion account does seek to recall to our mind this psalm, the previous verse is not mentioned: "They have pierced my hands and my feet; I can count all my bones" (Ps 22:17). In the psalm, the direct enemies of the sufferer divide up his garments, while in Mark 15:24 only his assigned executioners do so. Jesus is stripped of everything. Nothing is left to him, not his body, not his modesty, not the least consideration of any kind. He is reduced to total nakedness—absolute poverty.

Certain legal formalities remain to be seen to. The nature of the delict must be posted in plain view. And so, "the King of the Jews" (Mk 15:26) is inscribed and placed well on the cross for all to see. The joke, the demonstration of failure, could not have been more trenchant. Here is someone with nothing, someone who can do absolutely nothing, and he claimed to be a king. He had stood before his people and their leaders and claimed to be the Messiah. Jesus is reduced to nothing. His collapse has been a resounding one.

The original of Mark 15:26 is written in strange language. Literally, it reads: "And there was the inscription of his sentence inscribed," *kai ēn hē epigraphē tēs aitias autou epigegrammenē.* The word *epigraphē* occurs only twice in Mark: here and in 12:16—Caesar's "inscription" on the coin of tribute. Yes, the imperial "inscription," the seal of the empire's authentication, has struck back. The empire has had the last laugh. Jesus once demanded that we give ourselves to God wholly (Mk 12:17), with our whole life's strength (12:30). And Jesus is annihilated by the mighty Caesar.

On Jesus' left and right, outlaws were crucified with him (Mk 15:27)—his royal cortege. The collapse of his honor is complete.

Jesus is reduced to the level of the corrupt. This is how the powerful show what they think of him.

What sets Jesus at odds with the religious authorities is not simply a religious concept of the Messiah coupled with a particular political view. No, his religious Messiah is also political, and his politics is religious. The title "Son of David," which is equivalent to "King of Israel," has a religious sense (Mt 12:22–24; Mk 10:48). Jesus has had thrown up to him his alleged claim to be able to destroy the temple and quickly build another one, a better one. He has had thrown up to him his claim to be a Messiah, endowed with wisdom and mighty word, capable of prodigies and cures. Now, certain people mean to show, the facts have given him the lie (Berger 1974, 15). What has been done by torture is now reinforced with words. It is denied that Jesus has any relationship with God. It is demonstrated that Jesus is at odds with God.

Three groups of people taunt Jesus in this sense. First there are the "people going by" (Mk 15:29–30). Public execution by crucifixion was a spectacle, staged with a view to the total dishonor of the victim and the salutary admonishment of everyone else. Second are the priests and lawyers (15:31–32). Finally, he is taunted by the outlaws crucified along with him (15:32).

The first to insult him, after expressing their contempt, sarcastically add the reason: Jesus' claim to be great contrasted with the state of impotence in which he finds himself and from which he is challenged to extricate himself.

Those who pass by the way burst out laughing (Mk 15:29; cf. Ps 35:21) and wag their head or drop their jaws in token of profound contempt, as a sign of their delight, their gloating over the misery into which an enemy has fallen (cf. Sir 12:18). Theirs is the behavior of the haughty toward the poor (Pss 22:8, 109:25; Jb 16:4; Sir 13:7). Theirs is the reaction of the gentiles when Jerusalem finally lay in ruins (Jer 18:16; and especially Lam 2:15, with its striking similarity to inform the Markan passage). It is the classic affront to one who has nothing, who has been reduced to nothing.

In the mind of the "people going by," Jesus is demonstrating that his word is false, that his teaching is pure fairy tale. The one who promised to build a new and better temple—the one who thought himself capable of reforming in its very roots the institution that was most important to the people—cannot even extricate himself from his own miserable predicament. This is the meaning of "save" in Mark 15:30 (just as in 3:4, 5, 23, 28, 34, 6:56, 10:52). The cross is giving Jesus the complete lie.

In the evangelist's account the derision of Jesus is an offense against God (15:29). This brings us to the second series of insults as Chief Priests and lawyers come on the scene. The basic structure is the same as in verses 29-30. There is the deluge of words. Those who have until now been unable to find their tongue dissolve in waterfalls of contumely. And the one who has spoken surely clearly enough is now completely mute.

The "God-experts," those who know all about God and the Law, ridicule Jesus now. They approach Jesus swelling with might, drunk with power. They certainly "know what it is all about" (Schüngel 1974, 64). They know very well that what is at stake here is what Jesus has done for others: "He saved others," they say (Mk 15:31). But what he has done for a ruined people means nothing to them. Let him "save himself." Only this sort of power will bring them to "believe in him" (15:32). One who has descended to the cellar of society, who occupies the lowest rung on the social ladder, cannot speak or act in the name of God—not according to the God-experts. In their religious vision, it would be a contradiction for God to come to such a pass as this, to this situation of radical humiliation. And so they challenge Jesus to give them a sign (Mk 8:11-13, 11:28), something that will clearly show them that God's power is of the same class as that of the potentates and dominators.

Jesus makes no response to the demands of the religious authorities. His trust in God has other roots. His sense of God is totally different. Unlike Rabbi Jose ben Joezer, or even Isaiah in the Martyrdom of Isaiah 5:2-10, Jesus makes no response to the insults hurled at him (Pesch 1976, 2:490). Jesus' attitude is anything but in tune with the times.

These pious "men of God" are behaving toward Jesus just as the pagan soldiery has behaved (15:31; cf. 15:20). For Mark, as for the early Christian believers for whom he is writing, this religious vision deserves no more respect than does that of the godless ones (Ps 42:11) who deny that God is with the just or of those who would like to snatch from the people any relationship they may have with God (1 Mc 9:26; 2 Mc 7:10) or of the vain and corrupt persons who have persecuted the just one and who deny that the just one has anything to say to us about God (Wis 5:4, 2:12-16, 17-20).

Finally, Jesus is worthless even in the eyes of his fellow victims (Mk 15:32). Jesus is in the same condition as his people of old when they themselves seemed to have been abandoned by God (Is 37:3; Pss 89:51-52, 10:2-9).

What the Christians are suffering (Mt 5:11), rejected by all power, is what Jesus has suffered before them. Mark presents us with a Jesus rejected, despoiled, disfigured, and reduced to silence. He presents us with a laughingstock, a victim of the most shameful of deaths, one burdened with all the pain of the poor and the oppressed, one through whom God is revealed. This person "cut off from the land of the living" (Is 53:8) is the human face of God.

JESUS' DEATH

The taunts, the jibes, mount in intensity. No longer is it a matter for Jesus of verbal abuse—of having to listen to his claims being contrasted with his powerlessness (Mk 15:30), of having his ears ring with demands for a token of credibility and expressions of contempt for his inability to give one (15:31). No, the jeering is in deeds now. Bring on the wine and vinegar, and let the agony be prolonged. Even the victim's last prayer is mocked. It is important to demonstrate that here is a person dying completely abandoned by God (15:36-37) and receiving no heavenly aid. God fails to help him, either directly or indirectly through Elijah (15:35-36)—one of whose attributes was the consolation of the pious, the succor of the just in times of sorrow or need (Strack and Billerbeck 1922-28, 2:769-71).

Jesus dies in blackest solitude, in sheerest failure. He dies as one cursed by God, and nothing seems to suggest that he is not. He dies amid taunts and jeers of every kind, amid general rejection, without friends, without consolation, without having accomplished what he has undertaken, without a defender, with his cause discredited, and without any consolation of religion. Unlike the persecuted just one, Jesus cannot say, "The Lord has heard my plea; the Lord has accepted my prayer" (Ps 6:10; cf. Pss 10:14-15; 12:8-9; 13:8, 14:5-6; 17:15; 25:3). Jesus dies with a great cry of prayer, of supplication, of dire urgency (cf. Jdt 7:29, 9:1). His disciples gone, his work totally unappreciated, cast out from among his people, Jesus falls into the most profound helplessness possible to imagine. Jesus succumbs to death. Jesus dies absolutely and utterly dispossessed.

Totally and utterly condemned, humanly deprived of the faintest spark of hope. . . . Jesus turns to God. To the wise and the mighty, here is someone who no longer has any right to anything, and who indeed is deprived of everything. Precisely from within this nothingness, Jesus turns to God. The one who has been stripped of absolutely everything clings to God with all his might. The taunts and jeers, the demands for a sign that would strike a compromise with his tormentors' view of God—the established view of God—Jesus answers all this with a prayer. This prayer, uttered from the squalid depths of his misery, is the expression of his unshaken, unshakable faith (Pesch 1976, 2:495). From the depths of his total want of all things and his total aloneness . . . Jesus turns to God. Here is the extreme instance of faith, a faith stronger than Abraham's when he was about to sacrifice Isaac (Gn 22:1–14).

What Jesus' last words actually were has generated a great deal of discussion. But we are in the realm of speculation here. According to Luke, Jesus dies with the words, "Father, into your hands, I commend my spirit" (Lk 23:46). According to John, Jesus utters two phrases: "I am thirsty," and then, after he has been brought a sponge soaked in sour wine on the end of a hyssop, "Now it is finished" (Jn 19:28–30). In Mark, Jesus prays the opening verse of Psalm 22: "My God, my God, why have you forsaken me?" (Mk 15:34). Matthew appears to depend on Mark.

Actually, all three logia are quotations from or direct references to the Old Testament. What is more, each of the three logia corresponds exactly to the picture of Jesus proper to its respective Gospel. It would have been practically impossible for Jesus to recite an entire psalm in his condition. Nor, as it happens, is there anyone who could have reported—even roughly—what he said. The women who had come with him from Galilee were standing at some distance from the cross. Jesus was surrounded entirely by enemies and even their captain, as we shall see shortly, could have been unable to transmit Jesus' words faithfully. Finally, if any of these three reports were to be literally true, we would have the divergency of the other two to explain.

In the case of the logion Mark reports, there would be the further problem of explaining how the opening of such a familiar prayer, in which God's name is repeated and God is invoked, could have been confused with the simple invocation of Elijah, even if the "confusion" has been intentional. Of course, there could have been an abbreviation of the name Elijah (*Eliyyahu,* or *Eliyyah*) in the form of *Eli*—while at the same time the Aramaic word for the Lord God, *Elohi,* could hypothetically have sounded in a local dialect something like *Elhi,* or even *Eli* as in the Hebrew of the *Onchelos Targum* (Rehm 1958, 275). This could be. But we would still have the problem of how the rest of the phrase could have been so confused by the hearers when it was from a prayer as well known as this psalm.

The person who ran off to get the sour wine came back and said, "Now let's see whether Elijah comes to take him down" (Mk 15:36). The syllables Jesus had just pronounced must have sounded to him something like, "Come, Elijah!" or "Elijah is coming!" The latter phrase, which Sahlin retranslates into Aramaic as *Eliah ta,* would have indeed sounded almost exactly the same as *Eli atta,* or, "You are my God" (Sahlin 1952, 62). Indeed this is something Jesus might have prayed, for, as Léon-Dufour points out, the dying words of Rabbi Aqiba, the Jewish martyr, were, "The Lord is one"—that briefest possible, and traditional, résumé of Jewish faith (Léon-Dufour 1980, 162).

Then Jesus' death would represent the extreme case of "hoping against hope" (Rom 4:18), of absolute and unconditional abandonment to God. Utterly destroyed himself, Jesus demonstrates an indestructible trust in God. They have been able to take everything from him except his relationship with God. Everything has collapsed for him—except God.

None of the evangelists make any effort to give us a coroner's report on Jesus' death. The primitive church was not going to be able to live on curiosities of this kind. What it wanted and needed was to understand and hand on the meaning of Jesus' death. And this they did as they could, with the means available at their time and in their milieu.

We find a number of apocalyptic elements in the account of Jesus' death. Darkness covers the earth (Mk 15:33). Jesus cries out with a loud voice, the voice of someone revealing something at the moment of death (15:37). The veil of the temple sanctuary is rent asunder (15:38). We shall attempt to see the meaning of each of these elements.

The darkness is not a sign of mourning. If it were, it would have appeared at the moment of Jesus' death, or immediately afterwards. Instead it ends the moment Jesus dies. Darkness in the Old Testament is a symbol of death (see Jb 10:20–22), of massacre, of the crushing disgrace of the people at the hands of their God for their numberless crimes (Jer 11:16), of the tragic end of a people corrupted by injustice (Am 8:9–10), of the imminence of God's implacable, definitive justice (Is13:10, 24:13; Jl 2:2, 10, 3:4, 4:15; Rev 6:12–17). Jesus himself makes use of this symbolism (Mk 13:25). In other words, what we are being told in the passage before us is this: In Jesus' cross, the world has come to judgment, the world is this moment being judged.

Of course, a dust storm could have come up, driven by the desert winds, or perhaps a thunderhead. Only the evangelist is not a meteorologist, nor does he seek to be. Everything he writes, he writes in function of the good news—the way things have changed for us in Jesus Christ.

"Then Jesus, uttering a loud cry, breathed his last" (Mk 15:37), and this both puts an end to the darkness and is reported as the cause of the declaration of the centurion that Jesus is indeed the Son of God (15:39) (Betz 1964–76, 9:278–301). In Jesus' cry, uttered immediately before his death, the captain discerns a manifestation of extraordinary power (Stock 1978a, 294). In the Old Testament a loud voice, a "roaring" voice, is an expression of the divine sovereignty and might (Am 1:2; Hos 11:10; Jer 25:30; 1:24, 43:2; Rev 1:15). In death it is revealed what Jesus is, and this is what the centurion sees and then confesses (15:39). Jesus' cry has ushered in a new world (Léon-Dufour 1980, 167).

Between the time of Jesus' breathing his last (15:37) and the centurion's confession of faith, "the curtain in the sanctuary was torn in two from top to bottom " (15:38). This curtain served to close off the most sacred area of the temple (Ex 26:33). It was the "veil that [hung] before the ark" of the Covenant (Ex 30:6; 35:12; 40:3; Nm 4:5). Only the High Priest might enter the Holy of Holies, the part of the temple divided off by the curtain or veil, and then only once a year, on the Day of Atonement (Lv 16). It was a dark, windowless enclosure, and the dwelling-place of the Lord

(Lv 16:20; 1 Kgs 8:12; Ez 8:6) or of the Lord's "glory" (Ez 10:44). Here, then, was the glorious throne of God (Jer 14:21).

Jesus had predicted that the temple and all that it represented were seeing their last days (Mk 13:2; cf. 14:58, 15:30). The temple, with the type of religion it now stood for, had been turned into a "den of thieves" (Mk 11:17), a refuge for all manner of injustice. For Jesus the temple was irremediably corrupt. In killing Jesus, the temple administration had destroyed the temple's holiness, and so the veil that prohibited access to the Holy of Holies was rent asunder. The place had been profaned, violated. Within, nothing was to be found. The glory of the Lord (Ez 10) had fled, and this time for good. By expelling Jesus from their midst forever, the powers have prevented the manifestation of God's glory among them.

In order to be convinced of the symbolic nature of this rending of the temple curtain, we need only refer to the prodigies reported to have occurred at the death of a certain celebrated rabbi in Flavius Josephus' *Jewish War* (6:5 [1928], 294). On this occasion, the east gate of the temple, which twenty men could scarcely move, opened of itself in the middle of the night, precisely during the Passover celebration immediately preceding the outbreak of the Jewish War. Or we can recall something a little closer to home: the omens alleged to have occurred at the death of Tenochtilán. Prodigies reported at the death of rabbis always comported some symbolic biographical reference, either to the rabbi's life or to something special in his thought (Strack and Billerbeck 1922–28, 1:1041). Jesus' forte had been to break with exclusivist religion, a religion lashed to money, a religion of caste, a religion that conspired to "use" God for the purpose of amassing capital and influence. Jesus had been the enemy of all hard-heartedness, especially when it claimed to be in the service of God. With Jesus' death this asphyxiating world broke into smithereens.

As Paul Lamarche says, every great sign is polyvalent. Hence, in the case before us, the temple veil torn in two signifies two things: a final destruction and a final opening-up. The opening-up is the revelation of the mysteries of God (Lamarche 1979, 465–66). Jesus' death enables us to understand what God is and to approach God in a living, vital manner (He 10:19–22).

We must keep in mind that this account is being transmitted to us by someone who believes in Jesus' resurrection and who has found in that resurrection meaning for Jesus' death. Without this faith, the gospel writer would not have had the slightest interest in Jesus. This is also the case with the Christian community for whom the Gospel is being written, and this is what impelled them to seize upon Psalm 22 in order to describe Jesus' Passion (Gnilka 1978, 2:163).

The Psalms of Lamentation end in a prayer of thanksgiving. The purpose of their plaints is to celebrate God's salvific deed. Indeed, this is the purpose of laments addressed to God not only in the psalms but throughout the whole of the Old Testament.

We are told that, just before he died Jesus began to pray Psalm 22 with a loud cry—*eboēsen ho Iēsous phonē magalē* (Mk 15:34)—just as we hear the people (Ex 2:23; Nm 20:16; Jgs 10:10, 1 Sm 9:16), the poor person (Ex 22:21–22; Dt 24:15), and the just person who is poor did (Pss 22:2, 3, 6, 25: 69:14) in their extreme need, grief, or oppression.

In placing Psalm 22 on Jesus' lips, the first Christians are seeing Jesus as truly abandoned—just as abandoned as the oppressed and crushed people of the psalm. His grief, like theirs, is indescribable and scandalous. It is the pain of the poor, whose cry mounts to God, and to whom God cannot remain insensitive.

In these songs and stories God—all of whose power is committed to the side of the oppressed—is celebrated. The community that believes in Jesus, object of the cursing and vituperation of the great ones of this world, sees in Jesus the model of all the poor —trampled and destroyed—in whose favor God intervenes. In Jesus they see the defeat and the folly of the unjust, and, in turn, the victory of the one who reveals to us the true way to God (Wis 2:12–22). Before the cross of Jesus, the wisdom and grandeur of the mighty shatter into pieces (1 Cor 1:18–29).

At this level of interpretation, a level well beyond that of sheer grammatical or verbal interest, we can see that we are dealing with an involved, challenging account. It is an account that challenges us to make up our minds. Either we take Jesus for an imbecile for not accommodating to the ambitions and interests that are at stake here or else we recognize in him the strength and the wisdom of the divine love (1 Cor 1:23–24). Either we are as those who have condemned and excoriated Jesus or else we acknowledge him and follow him, cost what it may.

We have examples of the latter option in the centurion (Mk 15:39) and the women from Galilee (15:40). Seeing how Jesus had died, the centurion whose assignment it was to guard him said, "Clearly this man was the Son of God!" (v 39). The centurion grasped the whole character of Jesus' life in his death. It is in his death, as culmination of an entire life, that Jesus reveals what he is.

Sarcastic inquiry has been made as to what Jesus might be: the Messiah (Mk 14:61; 15:32), the Son of the blessed God (14:61), the King of the Jews (15:2,28), the King of Israel (15:32). Suddenly, in culmination of this whole process, it is affirmed in most emphatic fashion ("clearly," *alēthōs,* literally "truly," with the same force as in 14:70), that this individual, this person who has received the severest and most repulsive of all sentences, this person brought to the dust by the implacable logic of power, this person, precisely this person, is the Son of God—the one in whom God is revealed to us (15:39; cf. Wis 2:13, 6:6), the one in whom we discover the way to God (Wis 5:7). To look upon his life as folly and his death as shame (Wis 5:4) is to blind oneself to the truth (Wis 2:21–22) and to God's justice (Wis 5:6). To take such a view is to reject happiness itself (Wis 2:16).

With Jesus' death misunderstandings about him are at an end. He is the Son of God, yes, but this is not a title of power. On the contrary, it is a name—a manner of being, a way of living and existing—that has brought him into conflict with all the powers (Schüngel 1974, 65). "Son of God" is the ultimate expression of Jesus' identity in the Gospel of Mark. When Jesus dies, the veil of the temple sanctuary is torn asunder (Mk 15:38). In other words, with Jesus' death it is given to us to understand where God is, whose side God is on and whose against, how God is manifested, and to what God invites us and how. The pagan centurion, one of Jesus' torturers, a foreigner, a stranger "to the covenant and its promise . . . without hope and without God in the world" (Eph 2:12), discovers in the crucified Jesus the true face of God.

The God-experts and their hangers-on have been incapable of seeing God's manifestation in Jesus (Mk 15:32, 36). Peter, a disciple, denies knowing that a condemned prisoner called Jesus of Nazareth even exists (14:71). But in the way Jesus dies this pagan recognizes the road that leads to God (15:39).

It is only in the cross as a point of departure, then, according to Mark, that we can understand and discuss what Jesus really is. If we try to talk about him without the cross, we shall find all discourse about a unique relationship of his with God to be demoniacal (Mk 3:11, 5:7). To state this in less mythological terms, we can say that any consideration of Jesus that is not grounded in his rejection of the powerful is a blasphemous caricature of his person.

Neither Mark nor the church he represents has any reason to give us further details about the centurion, even his name. Their only concern is to place in his mouth what the community of believers has come to know and proclaim about Jesus of Nazareth who was crucified. For them, Jesus' good news (Mk 1:1) consists in this: This poor one called Jesus, hungering for bread and justice, passionately devoted to the oppressed, opposed to every sort of domination, free of all partisan interests, rejected by the great ones of the earth and their retainers to the point of being reduced to offal and malediction, is the very one who reveals the God of liberation to us. This good news is addressed to all. Indeed, in Luke's Gospel the centurion says, "Surely this was an innocent man" (23:47). He must never have become a Christian. Otherwise the apostolic community would not have had such difficulty in admitting other pagans (Acts 10:1-23).

Mark's Gospel tells us of three women who looked on from afar as Jesus was hanging on the cross (Mk 15:40). The disciples, those "reliable" males had disappeared. The last three to have been with Jesus had gone to sleep while their master was engaged in fierce interior struggles (14:33-42). Peter finally simply denied any knowledge of Jesus (14:66-72). The women who had followed Jesus had seen to his needs ever since they had left Galilee together (15:41). They had followed his steps right to the place of final confrontation and murder (10:1, 32-34, 46-52, 11:1-11). What the centurion professes in words they profess in deeds (Gnilka 1978, 2:327). They have understood that believing in Jesus means taking up his cross and following him (8:35). Weak and worthless as they were by prevailing standards, it is they who show what it is to be a disciple of Jesus and to live his message. They are a living illustration of Paul's vision of ecclesiality: "God chose those whom the world considers absurd to shame the wise; he singled out the weak of this world to shame the strong" (1 Cor 1:27).

These people make us understand what it means to be a Christian. Christian being is not exhausted in correct formulations of faith. Being a Christian means willingness to follow the cross. That is why it is only beneath the cross that one can clearly say for the first time, "This person was the Son of God" (Gnilka 1978, 2:170).

Surely at this point we shall "wag our heads," and judge not only this interpretation, but the core of the gospel itself, one great piece of foolishness. We shall by no means be the first to do so. The values of a paganism of old are only too like those of paganism today. Gods always look like big feudal lords. Here are three indissoluble concepts: god, domination, and money. No gods ever had any close ties with the oppressed. No one had ever found the gods hiding in the voice, the struggles, and the fate of the oppressed. Celsus used to ridicule Christians as just plain unfortunates, and judged it ridiculous that the Son of God should have been sent to a people as insignificant as the Jewish people (Origen, *Contra Celsum* 6:78, 3:55 [1953], 391, 165–66). Lucian called the Christians "poor devils" for denying the Greek gods (for denying the values of the dominant classes), for adoring this wretched sophist of theirs who was crucified, and for living according to his laws (Lucian, *De Morte Peregrini* 11–13 [1936], 12–15). All Jesus would have had to do, according to Celsus, was to prove his divinity by suddenly disappearing from the cross.

The cross and its meaning were the target of pagan ridicule, then. The cross was also an occasion of scandal for the Jews (1 Cor 1:24). The temple authorities, the recognized professors of the Law, could admit no close affinity between God and the shamed and dispossessed. Trypho put it this way to Saint Justin Martyr: "But whether Christ should be so shamefully crucified, this we are in doubt about. For whosoever is crucified is said in the law to be accursed, so that I am exceedingly incredulous on this point" (Justin Martyr, *Dialogue* 89 [1885], 224).

It is a new language—but it is the "same old warmed-over cat"—that faith today is called the enemy of progress. Of course, what is called progress obliterates persons, peoples, and nature itself. It is a "progress" and a "greatness" that simply buys and sells persons, peoples, and nature wholesale. This type of progress leads us to decomposition, destruction, and the slavery of lies, fear, and death. The only escape from this decay and this slavery is to accept the love of God revealed in Jesus—to believe in Jesus Christ. There is a victory over death: Jesus of Nazareth, with his life, his death, and his resurrection. In these he announces to us the good news of his victory. It is interesting to note that the first deviation from the apostolic tradition was the denial that Jesus Christ really lived and died a true human being.

The account of the Passion ends with the burial scene (Mk 15:42-47). The intense tone tells us "it's all over." The most frequently repeated words are "body," or "corpse" (15:43, 45, 46 [twice]), "died," "dead" (v 44 [twice], 45 [by allusion]), and "shroud," "linen" (v 46 [twice]). The end of the scene is dominated by "tomb" (vv 46, 47). By now Jesus' body is a mere object. It is taken down, wrapped (v 46), and placed in a tomb (vv 46, 47). Jewish law forbade the burial of delinquents like Jesus, the "godless," in family tombs. The bodies of such persons had to be thrown into a common ditch and left to decompose (Sanhedrin 6:5-6). Mourning was likewise prohibited.

The chief Roman executive, whose palm was well greased, in his "benevolence" (perhaps on some feast day in honor of Caesar) could grant the body of the person who had been executed to the family members, if they dared ask the favor. Neither a disciple nor a member of Jesus' family asked for Jesus' body. A person little known by the primitive Christian community did—Joseph, from Arimathea, a wealthy local judge, who "looked forward to the reign of God," to the fulfillment of the messianic promises (Mk 15:43; cf. Lk 2:25, 38). Joseph made bold to ask Pilate for Jesus' body (Mk 15:43) as only a rich person with a public charge like his could approach the governor with safety and confidence. The Roman authorities granted such a request only rarely. Besides, taking such an initiative could scarcely gain the petitioner favor with the local authorities. It is not clear why Joseph took this remarkable initiative.

Pilate was surprised that Jesus had already died (Mk 15:44). Generally a victim hung on the cross two or three days before dying. But Jesus had been accused of insurrection and hence had suffered more cruel torments than most of those condemned to crucifixion. It must be remembered that he had been so debilitated by his scourging that he had been unable to shoulder his cross (15:21) (Charlesworth 1972-73, 150).

Pilate granted Joseph the body (15:45)—Pilate, who had been so eager to remain on good terms with the Jewish authorities and the mob that he had handed over Jesus' living body to torture and death (15:15). It is hard to imagine anything more servile. Now he plays the great lord, granting Joseph Jesus' dead body, which he had sentenced while it was still alive.

There is a reason why the vocabulary of death is so insistent here. The Christian community had to face allegations that Jesus had been seen alive after Passover simply because he had not actually died, but had been taken down from the cross by his disciples and nursed back to health (Pesch 1976, 2:511).

Once more, the women stood afar, watching. They watched where the body of Jesus was laid to rest. They were to be the witnesses of this key element of the Christian message—that Jesus had really died—just as they were to be the witnesses that he had really risen. It so happened that in their society women's testimony had no validity. And so it might seem that the story of Jesus of Nazareth was over.

Chapter 7

The Resurrection

DIFFERENCES IN THE ACCOUNTS

Mark's account of Jesus' Resurrection is not only brief in the extreme, it also contains elements that disconcert us, especially if we try to read it as some sort of affidavit or biographical report. If we compare Mark's resurrection account and that of the other gospels, certain differences stand out. In John's Gospel, Jesus' body is laid to rest in accordance with Jewish usage—wrapped in cloths, with preservative spices (Jn 19:39–40); in Mark's Gospel the women come to Jesus' tomb precisely in order to place the spices with the body (Mk 16:1). Mark's Gospel has three women; Matthew's (18:1) has two; Luke's (24:1) has the women who had accompanied him from Galilee (Lk 8:1–3)—several, then—and John's (20:1) has but one. In John 20:2, Mary Magdalene runs to tell Peter and Jesus' favorite disciple what has happened; in Luke 24:9 the women tell the Eleven and everyone else everything; and in Mark 16:8 "they said nothing to anyone."

Further, even within the Markan text we encounter seemingly contradictory data. The women leave for the tomb "very early, just after sunrise, on the first day of the week" (Mk 16:2). And yet it has just been stated that they went out "when the sabbath was over," meaning, just after the sabbath rest (16:1). The women had seen where Jesus had been laid to rest, so they must have seen the stone rolled up to cover the entrance to the tomb. They had no way of rolling it away but were not even concerned about this until they had started out for the tomb (16:3). Besides, the phrase with which they express their belated anxiety is copied from 15:46. However, if Joseph of Arimathea had been able to move the stone by himself (15:46), why could not two women have done so? What the mysterious youth tells the women at the tomb is the same in content and form as what Peter and the other apostles would be preaching in Jerusalem (Acts 2:22–24, 3:15, 4:10, 5:30, 10:40, 13:30): The stranger speaks to the women of Jesus as the Nazarene and as the one who has been crucified (Mk 16:6), as if they did not know he was either. Jesus' associates have never referred to him as the Nazarene. Mark 16:7 not only seems to echo 14:28 where Jesus says, "I will go to Galilee ahead of you," but it does not entirely fit the context as the women do not then proceed to hand on the divine message but flee in terror and say "nothing to anyone" (16:8).

HEART AND SOUL IN THE TELLING

Nowhere in Mark's Gospel do we ever find a sober, detached account of anything Jesus said or did. Nothing is ever reported to us for the sheer objective satisfaction of reporting. This is eminently true of the Resurrection account. The members of the primitive church never spoke of the Resurrection in a detached, uncommitted way. They spoke of it with emotion and involvement (Schlier 1970, 10). Accordingly, we should here seek to understand how the Evangelist understands this divine occurrence and how he hopes to explain to us what God is telling us in it. The evangelist availed himself of the concrete means at his disposal. As Heinrich Schlier put it, the Resurrection accounts were redacted against a background of the thought-world of the time, and hence in the images, pictures, forms, ideas, and language of the world of that time and place (Schlier 1970, 13).

Thus there is no better way to understand what the evangelist meant to convey than to go at the text with compass and tweezers and see how it is put together. We are not denying its truth. We are only seeking to avoid boxing it into our molds and making it say things it never claimed to say.

STRUCTURE OF MARK'S ACCOUNT

After an introduction, the Markan acccount of Jesus' Resurrection contains three well-defined parts, marked off by the aorist feminine plural participle of the verb *erchesthai,* "to go," or its cognates: (1) the women go to the tomb (Mk 16:1), (2) they enter the tomb (16:5), (3) they leave the tomb (16:8).

The account also contains other key words which help give it its structure: *tomb, see, say,* and *wonder.* Here is how these four key words operate:

   I. The Tomb:
      A. The tomb is the goal of the women's journey (16:2)
      B. Seemingly it cannot be entered (v 3)
      C. The women enter it nonetheless, and find a surprise (v 5)
      D. They do not find what they expect to find (v 6)
      E. The women are shown that the tomb is empty (ibid.)
      F. They run away (v 8)
  II. Seeing:
      A. The women see the stone rolled back (16:4)
      B. They see a youth dressed in white, seated on the right (v 5)
      C. They do not see Jesus, and they perceive his absence by virtue of the empty tomb (v 6)
      D. They are told it is not they, but Peter and the disciples, who will see him later (v 7)
 III. Saying:
      A. The women "were saying to one another, 'Who will roll back the stone for us from the entrance to the tomb?'" (16:3)
      B. The youth tells them what has become of Jesus (v 6)
      C. The women are to tell Peter and the disciples what has happened (v 7)

    D. What has happened is what Jesus had said
       would happen (v 7)

    E. But they say nothing to anyone (v 8)

    F. The women begin their journey speaking with
       one another, but finish it in silence (16:3, 8)

IV. Wondering:

    A. The women experience no wonderment at
       seeing the stone already rolled back from the
       tomb (16:4)

    B. They are surprised and frightened, however,
       at the sight of the youth (v 5)

    C. He asks them to cease from their amazement
       (v 6)

    D. At the youth's message, the women are seized
       by fright and confusion, and fear reduces
       them to silence (v 8).

We have here a crescendo of fear and amazement. The synthesizing matrix of the whole verbal field of the account, of course, is: "He has been raised up; he is not here" (16:6) (Niemann 1979, 199). This is the center of everything. The verbs *see, speak, go,* and *wonder* or *amaze,* along with the frequent mention of the *tomb,* all occur in function of this one phrase, without which the story would make no sense.

This kernel, this nucleus will have to be expressed in the literary *genre* common to the evangelist's milieu. Let us repeat—for we are accustomed to think of the gospels as films of the life of Christ or as stenographic transcriptions of what an angel whispered in an evangelist's ear—let us repeat that we are not dealing here with a detailed report of the mechanics of Jesus' rising. We are dealing with an explanation of what the evangelist and the community to which he belonged and for which he wrote understood and lived by this "marvelous work of God."

SIMILAR FORMS

It is interesting to note the similarity between Mark's account and the account of the deliverance of the apostles from prison in Acts (5:22–25, 12:6–10). It was "during the night" that the angel "opened the gates" of the jail and "led them forth" (Acts 5:19). The "iron gate leading out to the city . . . opened for them of itself" (12:10). "During the night" Peter had been "sleeping . . . fastened with double chains" (12:6). It was also at night that the stone was rolled from the entrance to the tomb of Jesus.

The angel "woke" Peter (*egeiren*, Acts 12:7). Jesus had been "raised up," literally, "awakened" (*egerthe*, Mk 16:6). When the guards opened the jail they found no one within (Acts 5:23). Nor did the women find Jesus within the tomb. Someone said to the high priests, "Those men you put in jail are standing over there in the temple" (Acts 5:25). The angel says to the women: "You are looking for Jesus of Nazareth, the one who was crucified. He has been raised up; he is not here. . . . He is going ahead of you [Peter and the disciples] into Galilee" (Mk 16:6–7).

Jesus' Resurrection was a liberating deed of God. God snatched him from the prison of death. God utterly sets at naught the destructive deed of the dominant groups. This was also the conception held by the church in its first preaching: "God freed him from death's bitter pangs, however, and raised him up again, for it was impossible that death should keep its hold on him" (Acts 2:24).

The Markan account of the Resurrection, leaves us in the dark as to who rolled the stone away from the entrance to the tomb or how it was done. It was not rolled away for the women to enter—it had already been moved when they arrived. What might seem unexplained carelessness on their part (Mk 16:3) and afterthought (the size of the stone—16:4) is really a way of emphasizing how little prepared the women were for the Resurrection (Brändle 1967, 181). The deed has been one of God's deliverance, God's liberation, and hence it surpasses our wildest hopes.

Schlier said long ago: "The representation of angels in an empty tomb, a figure of the divine assistance, has its contemporary and biblical parallels" (Schlier 1970b, 13). We certainly do find the standard elements for the description of an angelic or divine manifestation:

1. The angelic garb: cf. 2 Maccabees 3:26–33, 5:2; and especially Daniel 7:9
2. The terror at the vision, the sight: cf. Exodus 3:6, 19:6; Isaiah 6:5; Ezekiel 1:28; Daniel 10:7–8

3. The exhortation to remain calm: cf. Judges 6:23; Deuteronomy 10:12
4. The announcement itself, the revelation—the central focus of all celestial manifestations
5. The confirmatory sign: cf. Exodus 3:12; Judges 6:38–40
6. The command: cf. Exodus 3:10; Judges 6:14, 23; Isaiah 6:9–10; Ezekiel 2:3
7. Fear at what has just been revealed: cf. Genesis 28:17; Judges 6:22; Deuteronomy 7:15, 28, 8:17, 27, 10:7–8
8. The silence: cf. Deuteronomy 7:15, 28, 10:15, 12:4
9. The flight: cf. Deuteronomy 10:7

We need not be surprised, then if, after the supreme revelation, the disciples reject the news. Nor should we see anything incongruous in the women's silence. Nor, finally, need we wonder about some "lost conclusion" to this Gospel, some hypothetical logical ending that would seem to be "missing."

Note that no one saw the stone being rolled back, let alone Jesus' actual Resurrection. We only know of these happenings through the witness of the church, which understood that, in professing its faith in the risen Jesus, it was acting as the instrument of God's revelation (Léon-Dufour 1971, 171). The youth dressed in white and seated on the right (but on the right of what or whom?), along with the fact that never in the whole of the Old Testament did a single divine messenger ever pronounce a revelation seated (Ammassari n.d., 124), simply conspire to confirm us in our feeling of being confronted with the symbols of theological reflection (Murphy-O'Connor 1969, 433).

Rudolf Pesch has pointed out the striking similarity between Mark's account and the other narratives of a fruitless search in which the person who has been taken up to heaven or raised from the dead "is not here"—this person now belongs to another reality. Among the instances he cites: Elijah in 2 Kings 2:16–18, Enoch in the Septuagint version of Genesis 5:24 and in Hebrews 11:5, Zechariah in the so-called Protoevangelium of Nicodemus (17:1), and especially in the apocryphal Testament in Job (39:40) with regard to Job's children (Pesch 1976, 2:522–27).

Accordingly, there is a literary need here to have the women wish to anoint Jesus' body in order to have the fruitless search. Both the discovery of the empty tomb and the announcement of a future manifestation of Jesus fulfill an important narrative function.

With these data, there is no need to chop the account to pieces and attribute to some half-verse the quality of "original core," while labeling everything else adventitious. Nor is there any reason to postulate the celebration of the Resurrection at a particular tomb. The basis and cause of the Resurrection account is the primitive community's faith in the bodily Resurrection of Jesus. In the spirit and mentality of his time and place, Mark has sought to explain the meaning and scope of the Resurrection for all of us.

NO RISING WITHOUT A PASSION

Some scripture scholars point out that without a knowledge of the burial account (Mk 15:42–47), we would not be able to grasp the basic data of the Resurrection account (16:1–8). For example, the women refer to Jesus by using the simple personal pronoun. Again, the women's conversation in 16:3 presupposes a knowledge of how the tomb was sealed (15:16). Even the walk to the tomb presupposes a knowledge of where it was (15:46). The indication made by the angel to the women (16:6) presupposes that they had seen where the body had been laid (Pesch 1976, 2:519).

The Rising of the Accursed One

These connections immediately suggest the impossibility of understanding the Resurrection without the Passion. It is not just anyone who is raised from the dead. It is Jesus the Nazarene, the one who was crucified (Mk 16:6). The women expect to see a corpse and see none. Never will Jesus' presence be the one they seek that morning, never more. Jesus is not a corpse; Jesus is not the prisoner of death. Jesus the Nazarene, the insignificant poor one who was crucified, the one rejected and destroyed as the lowest of the low, this threat to public order and incorrigible enemy of the manipulators and the mighty has been rescued by God from all power of destruction and corruption forever. God's future becomes present in this poor, destitute, disfigured, annihilated reprobate. This human being who was made into society's refuse has within him the life of God. The power of injustice and ambition, deceit, destruction, oppression, and money are rendered impotent before the life of God, the life that takes sides with the poor and the just.

Today is the first day of a new creation. The sun rises (Mk 16:3) in the darkness that has covered the earth (15:33). Light, new life, come to us from the risen Jesus (Eph 5:14; cf. Justin's *Apology* 1, 47). This Jesus, misunderstood, taken for insane, attacked, threatened, condemned, and murdered, is the same Jesus that has been raised again. This is what the titles given him by the youth, with the indication of the empty tomb, are meant to convey to us. It is the actual, earthly Jesus to whom this has happened, and Mark makes sure he is identified. For it is only thus that the name of Jesus and the title of Son of God can be the consolation of actual, mortal men and women. Only thus can we follow Christ (Pokorny 1973, 124).

Invalid Testimony

The women are entrusted with a message for Peter and the disciples. The persons considered the least capable, the ones whose testimony has no validity, are entrusted with carrying the first message of the risen Christ. The message with which they are entrusted is not directly that Jesus is risen, but that he is to fulfill a promise he made before he died. They only see the empty tomb. They do not speak with Jesus. Peter and the other disciples will see him personally and speak with him (Niemann 1979, 199).

Call to the Deserters

Peter and the other disciples may have deserted Jesus, but they will follow him once more (Schweizer 1967, 215). Faith in the risen Jesus forms a new community, a community of the forgiven. A group of hopeless cowards, whom Jesus seeks to infect with the strength of his new life, is remolded now. Peter, who has solemnly denied Jesus, will be for him now what Elisha once was for Elijah (2 Kgs 2:9–14) (see Pesch 1976, 2:534).

AN UNPREDICTABLE GOD

The women's reaction is one of stupor, trembling, confusion, flight, and silence. Fear has seized them utterly. They only expected to see Jesus' body, and sought to render him posthumous homage. Confronted with the unexpected, the humanly inconceivable, confronted with what the too narrow confines of their hope —confronted with this, the supreme deed of God, they feel literally unhinged. God is plucking them—as God is plucking us—from the narrowness, from the tight constraints of their lives. No pedestrian truth, this. This is the triumph of love and justice, the absolute guarantee of the triumph of life that God is communicating.

Confronted with the presence of God in the works and teachings of Jesus (Mk 1:27; Lk 5:29)—faced with the revelation of a power of God so contrary to the destructive powers of the human beings (Mk 10:24)—the crowds and the disciples have been stupefied again and again. The women's reaction could scarcely be any different. Nor can ours. We have come face to face with the crowning deed of God's power, the promise and guarantee that not all the powers of this world put together can destroy God and the chosen poor of God.

When Jesus restored the daughter of Jairus the synagogue official to life, those at the wake were filled with confusion (Mk 5:42). Yet this was only a partial triumph for life. At God's definitive victory, then, the confusion must be superhuman. Therefore Mark splashes his ink hither and yon, he multiplies his expressions of disproportion—of the dumbfounding wonder of it all, of the total, wild unexpectedness of the divine action. What God reveals to us in Jesus' Resurrection is something that language cannot exhaust, something the mind cannot get control of. God is always greater than our understanding and always greater than our heart.

The disciples did not wish to follow Jesus to Jerusalem. After all, that was the way of the cross. And indeed, once there, they abandoned him. When he was at the mercy of the oppressors, they fled (Mk 14:52). Now the women flee when the Resurrection is announced, as if this were a danger beyond their strength (5:14, 13:14). God's mystery is simply insupportable for human shoulders, and God's word at first shuts the mouths of those who should be bearing witness to God (Radermakers 1973, 76).

Not only his enemies and the crowds, but even the disciples failed to understand Jesus. They were incapable of seeing his life as the full revelation of God. Mark's Gospel emphasizes this incomprehension again and again. This is the way of telling us that, by themselves alone, men and women are incapable of understanding and seeing as God understands and sees. If there is anything that explodes our categories into thin air—to paraphrase Jean Delorme—it is the mystery of the Resurrection of Jesus the Nazarene, who was crucified. This is the heart of the gospel (Delorme n.d., 134).

LIBERATION FROM EVERY ENCUMBRANCE

The disciples and the crowds, seeing in Jesus the manifestation of the divine power which vanquishes whatever destroys persons (Mk 4:41, 5:15, 33) or lords it over nature (6:50), were filled with fear. Now fear in the face of Jesus' Resurrection reduces the women to silence. The gospel is not a good news that the human spirit can accept without profound confusion. What will overcome this confusion? The message of an angel? No. The reading of the gospel? No. One can only be still, and await the enlightenment of God in person (Léon-Dufour 1971, 197).

As he closes his Gospel, Mark invites us to feel the fascination of a new life, a life which shed its light on us and delivers us from the narrow confines of our finite perspective (Pesch 1976, 2:152). He invites us to think about, wonder about, react to, the divine message of the raising of the poor one, Jesus of Nazareth, who was condemned and crucified. He invites us to live by faith in this liberating power of God. He invites us to join the group of "the disciples, and Peter," where this faith will fill our lives with value and gladness.

TRIUMPH OF LIFE

An analysis of the passage dealing with the Resurrection shows how easily they lend themselves to a variety of interpretations. It is impossible to remain neutral before this phenomenon. The conclusions we draw will be determined by the meaning we give to "neighbor" and to "God." Our interpretation of the Resurrection will depend on the type of life we seek—on the degree of nearness to, or distance from, Jesus' struggles that we seek—on what we have accepted of his life.

Acceptance or rejection of Jesus' Resurrection is not a matter of sheer intelligence or understanding. It demands a vital, living decision. It involves a perpetual sides-taking behavior, a persistently committed manner of conduct. Therefore I have no wish to cover anything up. I shall now throw all my cards on the table.

Jesus did not die a natural or accidental death. Jesus was murdered. He was not murdered by an uncontrollable mob or by a gang of thugs. He was murdered by the enlightened, decent, respectable people of his time. Jesus was murdered by the powerful. Jesus died calumniated, betrayed, tortured, and deserted. He was not killed for entering into intrigues. He was killed for having stymied all power. He was not killed because he was unjust. He was killed because he unmasked all "justice" whose goal was other than meeting the needs of the poor.

Jesus was murdered for altering the established order, for being a danger to the state. Above all he was murdered for blaspheming—for being the sworn enemy of God. The dominators of consciences, the exploiters of the people, could not temporize with Jesus. More than this: Jesus, without weapons, ambushes, or intrigues, was destroying their peace. Jesus was destroying their whole moral and religious basis for oppressing, or even for remaining aloof from, others. Jesus' order, hope, and sense of God were in direct, irreconcilable opposition to those of the dominant groups.

The God of Jesus is a God of life, a God involved with the oppressed and committed to them, the strength and joy of the crushed and the outcast. God will brook no inequalities. God's cause is the cause of the poor, and God's self is revealed in the face of the poor person. Jesus proclaims a God who is near the suffering, who is the strength that raises the oppressed from the dust, who is the worth of the humiliated. That God is the radical rejection of all oppressive power and is divorced from exploitation and the accumulation of money.

The reign of God, the center of Jesus' message and the reason for his conduct, implies an about-face in the political, economic, and religious situation. God is not only an appeal to conscience but is also a challenge to believe in, and to create, the future. God is the one who "has deposed the mighty from their thrones and raised the lowly to high places." God is the one who to the poor "has given every good thing, while the rich he has sent empty away" (Lk 1:53).

Jesus does not maintain the status quo nor bestow a little bit of consolation. Jesus proclaims the presence of the reign of God. A radical change is feasible in this life! God's justice can be lived right here! *Here* God seeks to liberate human beings!

Jesus' values, Jesus' hopes, and Jesus' sense of God are different, and he hands these to us. They are the contrary of those inculcated by all the oppressors. The oppressors, in ridding themselves of Jesus, sought to do away with all identification of God's cause with the cause of the oppressed. They had hoped to preserve the notion of a God whose back was turned on the pain of the poor. They sought to abort a promise or future, for the humiliated and despoiled. They tried to snatch God from the struggles, the sorrow, and the hearts of the poor. In killing Jesus they sought to kill any subversive power residing in *faith in God*—God the liberator and comrade of the exploited and the sinners. They thought they could lay to rest the conflict unleashed by Jesus by laying him to rest in the tomb.

Jesus was rejected because he was poor and the liberator of the poor. He was rejected for being the revelation of a God committed to the poor. If we fail to keep in mind the cause of Jesus' rejection and murder, we shall be unable to grasp what the gospels are trying to say when they speak to us of Jesus the poor carpenter from Nazareth who is risen from the dead. Throughout the gospels, God is revealed to us in Jesus as a force contrary to and superior to the power of oppression and money. In killing Jesus, his enemies hoped to cloud this manifestation of the power of the living God.

The great question that we must put to ourselves as we behold Jesus' death is this: Can the God who has been revealed to us in Jesus be bound, completely paralyzed, by the powers of oppression? Is this a God who is routed and defeated in the face of the pain of the oppressed and is helpless to alleviate it? We can begin to answer our question with this statement: If Jesus has a future, then nothing, and no one, can prevent the future, the definitive triumph, of the oppressed. This world, this disfigured, crushed corporeal reality, has something really new in store: "new heavens and a new earth" (Rev. 21:2), where justice shall reign. Nothing can prevent

God's full manifestation in history, however much this history may be the constant scene of cruelty and crime.

This proposition has nothing romantic or escapist about it. It springs up as a dramatic demand from Jesus' actual conduct. In order to help the reader appreciate the solid practicality of this proposition, allow me to cite a well-known author whose Christian orthodoxy may leave something to be desired. Lenin once wrote that there were two kinds of daydreams. One kind can actually come true; the other kind cannot. The first kind of daydreaming, he said, is actually good for us. Far from paralyzing effort, it motivates it. Indeed, if the human being were unable to dream dreams like these, there would be no vast and arduous enterprises and accomplishments such as those we behold in the arts, the sciences, and practical life. When life has a contract with dreams, said Lenin, that is a good omen (Dri 1979, 170). To posit the factual reality of Jesus' Resurrection is not to take refuge in daydreams. It is simply to wonder about a force that will generate an irreversible and unlimited liberation process.

Does Jesus' life comport an irrepressible explosion of hope? Does it present an alternative for the oppressed? Is it the experience of a God of boundless love, or is it merely the satisfaction of a bourgeois conscience? Will the liberation of the oppressed in the good news brought by Jesus only go so far? Will the power of destruction and death be history's last and definitive word? Will God be nothing but a palliative for invincible injustice and the irremediable evil of death? Can anything render the struggle for the radical liberation of all the oppressed irrepressible? Can anything guarantee the complete triumph of life?

Truly, to pose the problem of Jesus' Resurrection is to pose the problem of God in its ultimate consequences. The North Atlantic exegetes posit their theses. Rudolf Bultmann, for example, holds that "the meaning of the Paschal faith is to believe in Christ present in the church's proclamation." But Bultmann does not mean a Christ who is identical with Jesus. Jesus, after all, is dead. Willi Marxsen says: "We continue to be challenged by what Jesus did and said." But of course Jesus is past tense and purely exemplary. If you examine these ideas closely, you see that they are unintelligible and irrelevant for the poor. Therefore they must correspond to concerns very different from those of the gospel texts. More specifically, I fail to see how in these theories, a *body* means anything—especially a body tortured and disfigured by the brutality of toil or destroyed by hunger.

Only in a struggle and commitment like Jesus' struggle and commitment will the question of his Resurrection cease to be an idle question. The question has been posed authentically less by theologians or Bible scholars than by the priests and peasant apostles murdered by the government of El Salvador, by the sisters tortured by the inhuman, military governments of South America, by the native catechists massacred by the *criollo* oligarchies. Only in the living thesis of these kinds of persons can we grasp the meaning of the victory of God, of Jesus, over death.

Works Cited

Ambrozic, Aloysius. 1972. *The Hidden Kingdom*. Catholic Biblical Quarterly Monograph Series 2. Washington, D.C.: Catholic Biblical Association.

Ammassari, A. *La Resurrezione*. Cittadella.

Augustine. *Commentary on John*.

Behm, Johannes. 1964–76. "*Nestis*." In Kittel 1964–76.

Benoit, Pierre. 1968. "Les Epis arrachés." In *Exégèse et Théologie*. Paris: Cerf.

Berger, Klaus. 1970. *Die Amen-Worte Jesu: eine Untersuchung zum Problem der Legitimation in apokalyptischer Rede*. Berlin: de Gruyter.

———. 1974. "Zum Problem der Messianität Jesu." *Zeitschrift für Theologie und Kirche*. Vol. 74, no. 1.

Betz, Otto. 1964–76. "*Phōnē*." In Kittel 1964–76.

Beyer, Hermann Wolfgang. 1964–76a. "*Blasphēmeō*." In Kittel 1964–76.

———. 1964–76b. "*Eulogeō*——." In Kittel 1964–76.

Blinzler, Josef. 1969. *Der Prozess Jesu*. Regensburg: Pustet.

Brändle, M. 1967. "Musste das Grab Jesu leer sein?" *Orientierung*.

Bultmann, Rudolph. 1961. *Die Geschichte der Synoptischen Tradition: Forschungen zur Religion und Literatur der Alten und Neuen Testament*. Göttingen: Vandenhoeck & Ruprecht. English translation: *The History of the Synoptic Tradition*. 2d ed. Trans. John Marsh. New York: Harper and Row, 1963.

Capelle, A. 1975. Cited in *Lecture matérialiste de l'évangile de Marc: récit-pratique-idéologie*. Fernando Belo. Paris: Cerf. English translation: *A Materialist Reading of the Gospel of Mark*. Maryknoll, N.Y.: Orbis, 1981.

Charlesworth, J. H. 1972–73. "Jesus and Johanan: An Archaeological Note on Crucifixion." *Expository Times* 84 (no. 5): 147–50.

Cicero. *Pro Rabirio*. Chap. 5. In *Cicero: The Speeches*. Trans. H. Grose Hodge. The Loeb Classical Library. London: Heinemann; New York: Putnam, 1927.

———. *In Verrem*. Book 5, chap. 66. In *Cicero: The Verrine Orations*. Vol.

2. Trans. L. H. G. Greenwood. The Loeb Classical Library. Cambridge, Mass.: Harvard University Press; London: Heinemann, 1935.

Darrett, J. D. M. 1972. "Eating Up Houses of Widows: Jesus' Comments on Lawyers?" *Novum Testamentum* 14 (no. 1): 1-9.

Delorme. Jean. *La Resurrection du Christ et l'exégèse moderne.* Paris: Cerf.

de Vaux, Roland. 1961. *Les Institutions de l'Ancien Testament.* Paris: Cerf. English translation: *Ancient Israel: Its Life and Institutions.* New York: McGraw-Hill, 1967.

Dodd, C. H. 1976. *Historical Tradition of the Fourth Gospel.* Cambridge: Cambridge University Press.

Dri, R. R. 1979. *Insurrección y resurrección.* Centro de Estudios Ecuménicos. Citing Lenin, ¿*Qué Hacer?* Moscow: Progeso.

Dupont, Jacques. 1969. *Les Béatitudes.* Paris: Gabalda.

Eichrodt, Walther. 1961–67. *Theology of the Old Testament.* Trans. J. A. Baker. Philadelphia: Westminster.

——. 1966. *Der Prophet Hesekiel,* Das Alte Testament deutsch 22. Göttingen: Vandenhoeck & Ruprecht. English translation: *Ezekiel: A Commentary.* Trans. Cosslett Quin. Philadelphia: Westminster, 1970.

Elliger, Karl. 1956. *Das Buch der Zwölf Kleinen Propheten.* ATD 24/25. Göttingen: Vandenhoeck & Ruprecht.

Foerster, Werner. 1964–76. "*Diabolos.*" In Kittel 1964–76.

Gnilka, Joachim. 1978. *Das Evangelium nach Markus.* Evangelisch-Katholischer Kommentar zum Neuen Testament. Zurich: Benziger/ Neukirchener.

Gonzáles-Faus, José Ignacio. 1977. "Jesús y los demonios." *Estudios Eclesiásticos.*

Grundmann, Walter. 1962. *Das Evangelium nach Markus.* Berlin: Evangelische.

Hahn, F. 1976. In Pesch 1976.

Hansen, Günther. 1973. In Leipoldt and Grundmann 1973.

Hauck, Friedrich. 1964–76a. "*Katharos.*" In Kittel 1964–76.

——. 1964–76b. "*Moicheuō.*" In Kittel 1964–76.

Hauck, Friedrich, and Wilhelm F. Kasch. 1964–76. "*Ploutos.*" In Kittel 1964–76.

Hengel, Martin. 1971. *Was Jesus a Revolutionist?* Trans. William Klassen. Philadelphia: Fortress.

——. 1973a. *Judentum und Hellenismus.* Tübingen: J. C. B. Mohr. English translation: *Judaism and Hellenism.* Trans. John Bowden. Philadelphia: Fortress, 1981.

——. 1973b. *Victory over Violence: Jesus and the Revolutionists.* Trans. David E. Green. Philadelphia: Fortress.

——. 1976. "Mors Turpissima Crucis." In *Festschrift. Ernst Käsemann. The Interpreter's Bible*. 1951–57. New York: Abingdon.

Jeremias, Joachim. 1964–76a. "*Grammateus*." In Kittel 1964–76.

——. 1964–76b. "*Poimēn*." In Kittel 1964–76.

——. 1966. *The Eucharistic Words of Jesus*. Trans. Norman Perrin. London: SCM Press.

——. 1977. *Jerusalén en tiempos de Jesús*. Madrid: Cristiandad. English translation: *Jerusalem in the Time of Jesus*. Trans. F. H. and C. H. Cave. Philadelphia: Fortress, 1969.

Josephus. *The Jewish War*. Book 2, chap. 5. In *Josephus*. Trans. H. St. J. Thackeray. Vol. 2. *The Jewish War, Books I–III*. Loeb Classical Library. London: Heinemann; New York: Putnam, 1928.

——. *The Jewish War. Book 4. In Josephus*. Trans. H. St. J. Thackeray, Vol. 3. *The Jewish War, Books IV–VII*. Loeb Classical Library. London: Heinemann; New York: Putnam, 1928, pp. 150–53.

——. *The Jewish War*, Book 6, chap. 5. In *Josephus*. Trans. H. St. J. Thackeray. Vol. 3. *The Jewish War, Books IV–VII*. Loeb Classical Library. London: Heinemann; New York: Putnam, 1928.

Justin Martyr. *Dialogue with Trypho*. Chaps. 69 and 89. In *The Ante-Nicene Fathers*. Vol. 1. *The Apostolic Fathers with Justin Martyr and Irenaeus*. Ed. Alexander Roberts and James Donalson. New York: Christian Literature, 1885.

Justinian. *Digest of Roman Law*. Book 38, chap. 2; Book 48, chap. 19.

Kertelge, Karl. 1970. *Die Wunder Jesu im Markusevangelium*. Munich: Kösel.

Kittel, Gerhard, ed. 1964–76. *Theological Dictionary of the New Testament*. 10 vols. Trans. and ed. Geoffrey W. Bromiley. Grand Rapids, Mich., and London: Eerdmans.

Köster, Helmut. 1964–76. "*Splangchnizomai*." In Kittel 1964–76.

Lamarche, Paul. 1966. *Le Christ vivant*. Paris: Cerf.

——. 1979. "L'Humiliation du Christ." *Christus* (Paris).

Lee, G. M. 1971. "The Story of the Widow's Mite." *Expository Times* 82.

Leipoldt, Johannes, and Walter Grundmann, eds. 1973. *El mundo del Nuevo Testamento*. Madrid: Cristiandad.

Léon-Dufour, Xavier. 1964. *Etudes d'Evangile*. Paris: Seuil.

——. 1971. *Resurrection de Jésus et message pascal*. Paris: Seuil.

——. 1979. "Jésus à Gethsémani." *Science et Esprit* 3.

——. 1980. *Face à la mort: Jésus et Paul*. Paris: Seuil.

Lohse, Eduard. 1964–76. "*Sabbaton*." In Kittel 1964–76.

Lucian. *De morte Peregrini*, 11–13. In *Lucian. The Passing of Peregrinus*. Vol. 5. Trans. A. M. Harmon. The Loeb Classical Library. Cambridge,

134   *WORKS CITED*

Mass.: Harvard University Press; London: Heinemann, 1936.

Martini, Carlo M. 1971. "I Resti dell' uomo crocifisso ritrovati a Gib' at Ha-Mivtar." *Civiltà Cattolica.*

Menander. *Fragments* 794–95 (547–48). In *Menandri fragmenta quae supersunt.* Ed. Alfredus Koerte. Leipzig: Teubner, 1959.

Meyer, Rudolf. "*Pharisaios.*" In Kittel 1964–76.

———. "*Prophētēs.*" In Kittel 1964–76.

Minette de Tillesse, Georges. 1968. *Le Secret messianique dans l'Evangile de Marc.* Paris: Cerf.

Moulton, James Hope, and George Milligan. 1963. *The Vocabulary of the Greek New Testament.* Grand Rapids, Mich.: Eerdmans.

Mouroux, Jean. 1953. *Sens chrétien de l'homme.* Paris: Aubier. English translation: *The Meaning of Man.* New York: Sheed and Ward, 1948.

Muilenberg, James. 1951–57. "The Book of Isaiah." In *The Interpreter's Bible.* New York: Abingdon.

Murphy-O'Connor, J. 1969. Review of L. Schenke, *Auferstehungsverkündigung und leeres Grab. Revue Biblique* 43.

Niemann, F. J. 1979. "Die Erzählung vom Leeren Grab bei Markus." *Zeitschrift für Katholische Theologie.*

Nieri, Nora. 1929–39. "Croce." *Enciclopedia Italiana.* Rome: Instituto Giovanni Treccani.

Oepke, Albrecht. 1964–76. "*Gunē.*" In Kittel 1964–76. Citing Philo, *De specialibus legis,* III, 35.

Origen. *Contra Celsum.* Book 6, chap. 78; Book 3, chap. 55. In *Origen: Contra Celsum.* Trans. Henry Chadwick. Cambridge (England): University Press, 1953.

Pascal, Blaise. 1962. *Pensées.* Paris: Seuil. English translation: *Pensées.* Trans. A. J. Krailsheimer. Baltimore: Penguin, 1966.

Pesch, Rudolf. 1970. "Das Zöllnergastmahl: Mk 2." In *Mélanges bibliques en hommage au R. P. Beda Rigaux.* Gembloux: Duclot.

———. 1974. "Die Verleugnung des Petrus." In Schnackenburg 1974.

———, ed. 1976. *Das Markusevangelium.* Freiburg i.B.: Herder.

Plato, *Republic.* Book 2, no. 361. In *The Dialogues of Plato.* Trans. Benjamin Jowett. Great Books of the Western World 7. Chicago, London, Toronto: Britannica, 1952, p. 312.

Plautus, *Miles Gloriosus.* No. 359. *The Braggart Warrior.* In *Plautus.* Vol. 3. Trans. Paul Nixon. The Loeb Classical Library. London: Heinemann; New York: Putnam, 1930.

———. *Asinaria,* 940. In *Plautus.* Vol. 1. *The Comedy of Asses.* Trans. Paul Nixon. The Loeb Classical Library. London: Heinemann; Cambridge, Mass.: Harvard University Press, 1937.

Pokorny, Peter. 1973. *Die Kirche des Anfangs Benno.*

Radermakers, Jean. 1973. "Precher le Ressuscité." *Lumen vitae.*

Rehm, M. 1958. "'Eli, Eli, lamma sabactani.'" *Biblische Zeitschrift.*

Reicke, Bo. 1964–76. "*Chrēma.*" In Kittel 1964–76.

Rengstorf, Karl Heinrich. 1964–76. "*Harmartōlos.*" In Kittel 1964–76.

Reploh, Karl G. 1969. *Markus: Lehrer der Gemeinde.* Stuttgart: Katholisches Bibelwerk.

Rostovtzeff, Mikhail. 1941. *The Social and Economic History of the Hellenistic World.* Oxford: Clarendon.

Rudolph, William. 1968. *Jeremia.* Handbuch zum Altem Testament Series. Tübingen: J. C. B. Mohr.

Sahlin, H. 1952. "Zum Verständnis von drei Stellen des Markusevangeliums." *Biblica.*

Sallust. *Conspiracy of Catiline* 52. In C. Sallusti Crispi, *Bellum Catilinae.* Ed. Alfred Gudeman. New York: Appleton, 1904.

Schlier, Heinrich. 1970a. "El Estado en el Nuevo Testamento." In *Problemas exegéticos fundamentales del Nuevo Testamento.* Fax.

———. 1970b. "Sobre la resurrección de Jesucristo." *DDB.*

———. 1979. *Die Markuspassion.* Einsiedeln: Johannes.

Schnackenburg, Rudolph. 1971. "Die Ehe nach dem Neuen Testament." In *Schriften zum Neuen Testament: Exegese in Fortschritt und Wandel.* Munich: Kösel.

———. 1974. *Neues Testament und Kirche.* Basel: Herder.

Schneider, G. "Die Verhaftung Jesu." *Zeitschrift für Neutestamentliche Wissenschaft.*

Schüngel, P. H. 1974. "Die Erzählung des Markus über den Tod Jesu." *Orientierung.*

Schürmann, Heinz. 1969. *Das Lukasevangelium.* Freiburg i.B.: Herder.

Schweizer, Eduard. 1967. *Das Evangelium nach Markus.* Göttingen: Vandenhoeck & Ruprecht. English translation: *The Good News According to Mark.* Trans. Madvig Donald. Richmond: John Knox, 1970.

Seneca. *Of Consolation.* Book 6, chap. 20. In L. Annaeus Seneca, *Minor Dialogues.* Trans. Aubrey Stewart. London: Bell, 1889.

———. *De beneficiis* 3, 16, 2, 3. In Sénèque, *Des Bienfaits.* Paris: Belles Lettres, 1961.

Simon, L. 1969. "Le Sou de la veuve." *Etudes théologiques et religieuses.*

Sophocles. Fragment 488. In *The Fragments of Sophocles.* Ed. A. C. Pearson. Amsterdam: Hakkert, 1963.

Stauffer, Ethelbert. 1964–76. "*Gameō, gamos.*" In Kittel 1964–76.

Stock, K. 1978a. "Das Bekenntnis des Centurio." *Zeitschrift für Katholische Theologie.*

———. 1978b. "Gliederung und Zusammenhang in Mk 11–12." *Biblica,* 59, no. 4.

"Die *Stolai* der Schriftgelehrten: Eine Erklärung zu Mark 12:38." 1963. In *Festschrift Otto Michael: Abraham, unser Vater*. Leiden: Brill.

Strack, Hermann L., and Paul Billerbeck. 1922–28. *Kommentar zum Neuen Testament aus Talmud und Midrash*. Munich: C. H. Beck.

Tacitus. *Histories*. Book 4, chap. 11, ad fin. In P. Cornelius Tacitus, *The Annals and the Histories*. Great Books of the Western World 15. Chicago, London, Toronto: Britannica, 1952,

Tannehill, Robert C. 1975. *The Sword of His Mouth*. Philadelphia: Fortress.

Taylor, Vincent, ed. 1966. *The Gospel According to Saint Mark*. London: Macmillan.

Theissen, Gerd. 1978. *Sociology of Early Palestinian Christianity*. Trans. John Bowden. Philadelphia: Fortress.

Vanhoye, Albert. 1970. *De narrationibus passionis Christi in Evangeliis Synopticis*. Rome: Biblicum.

———. 1971. "L'Angoisse du Christ." *Christus* (Paris).

Vawter, Bruce. 1977. "Divorce and the New Testament." *The Catholic Biblical Quarterly* (October).

von Rad, Gerhard. 1967. *Théologie de l'Ancien Testament*. Labor et Fides. English translation: *Old Testament Theology*. 2 vols. Trans. D. M. G. Stalker. New York: Harper and Row, 1962–65.

Westermann, Claus. 1976. *Genesis, Kapitel 1–11*, K.A.T.I. Neukirchen: Neukirchener.

Wilckens, Ulrich. 1964–76. "*Stolē*." In Kittel 1964–76.

Windisch, Hans. 1964–76. "*Aspasmos*." In Kittel 1964–76.

Ziesler, J. A. 1973. "The Removal of the Bridegroom." *New Testament Studies* (January).